POLISH WIN

Lechosław Musiałkowski

Mikoyan Gurevich MiG-15 and Licence Build Versions

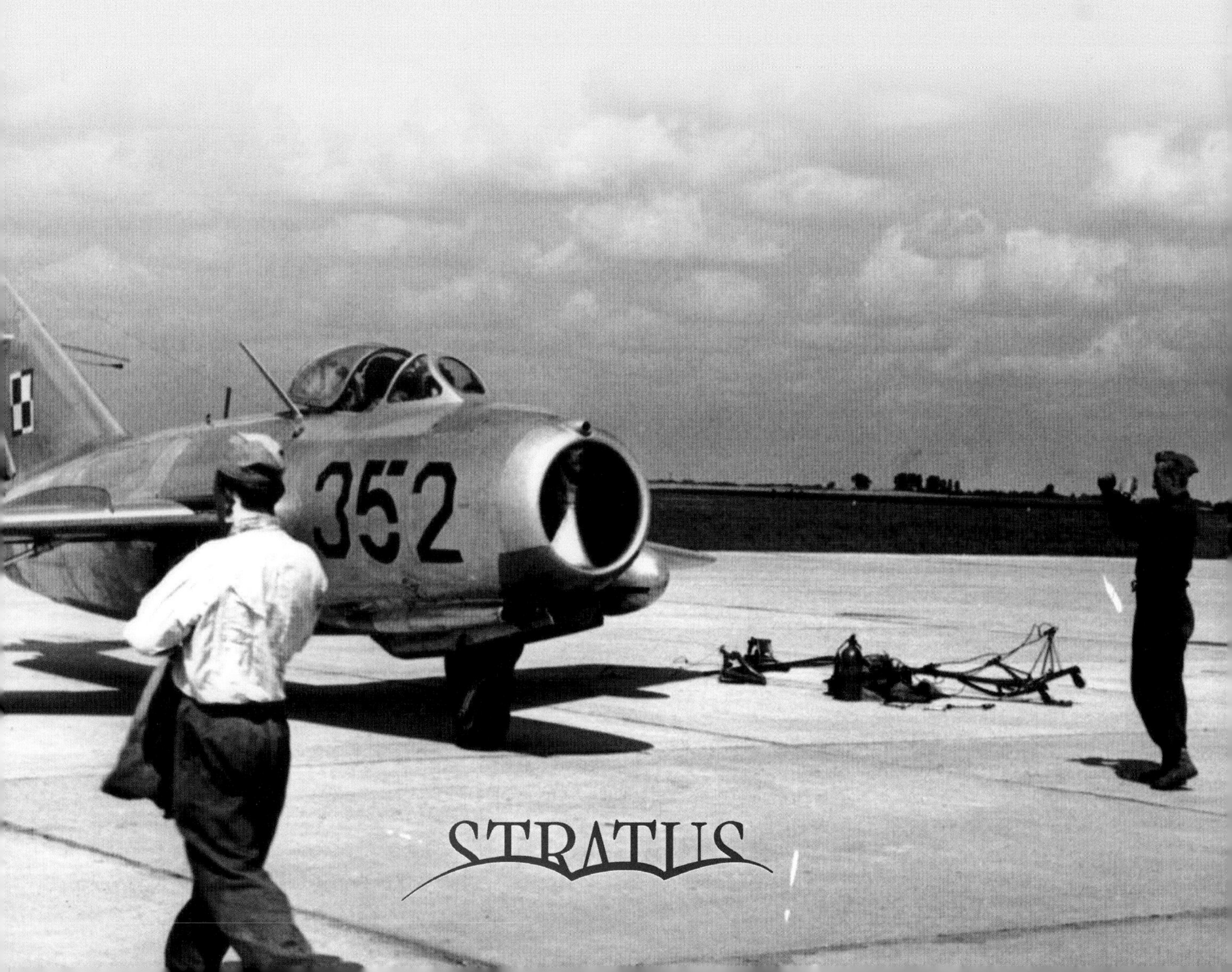

STRATUS

Wydawnictwo STRATUS s.j.
ul. Żeromskiego 4, 27-600 Sandomierz, Poland
phone. 0-15 833 30 41
e-mail: office@stratusbooks.pl
www.stratusbooks.com.pl www.mmpbooks.biz

ISBN 978-83-66549-92-0

Layout concept	Bartłomiej Belcarz
Cover concept	Artur Juszczak
Cover	Marek Ryś
Translation	Jarosław Dobrzyński
Proofreading	Roger Wallsgrove
DTP	Bartłomiej Belcarz Artur Juszczak
Colour Drawings	Andrzej M. Olejniczak
Edited by	Roger Wallsgrove

PRINTED IN POLAND

The author would like to thank the following persons and institutions for their assistance in his work on the book, and for providing photographs and documents:

Photo credits: Zbigniew Chmurzyński, Kazimierz Fijałkowski, Wacław Hołyś, Stanisław Iwan, Bernard Koszewski, Andrzej Morgała, Stanisław Syndoman, Janusz Szymański and Lech Zielaskowski.

Photographs are from archives of: Bartłomiej Belcarz, Jacek Borowiński, Mikael Forslund, Jerzy Gotowała, Robert Gretzyngier, Ryszard Grundman, Wacław Hołyś, Bolesław Jeska, Dariusz Karnas, Krzysztof Kirschenstein, Grzegorz Klimasiński, Mariusz Konarski, Anna M. Kotulska, Jerzy Kozarek, Andrzej Majewski, Wojtek Matusiak, Marian Mikołajczuk, Cezary Piotrowski, Wojciech Sankowski, Lucjan Sokólski, Henryk Sygnowski, Konrad Zienkiewicz, author, Instytut Lotnictwa and WAF.

The author would like to thank Bartłomiej Belcarz, Grzegorz Klimasiński, Krzysztof Kirschenstein, Wojtek Matusiak and Wojciech Sankowski for their help at various stages of this work.

Szczególne podziękowania dla Grzegorza Klimasińskiego, bez którego życzliwości i pomocy ta publikacja byłaby skromniejsza. Dziękuję Grześ.

In memory of 116 Polish airmen who died in crashes of the MiG-15 fighters and their licence versions.

Polish unit names and abbreviations and their English translations:
Korpus Lotnictwa Myśliwskiego (KLM) – Fighter Aviation Corps
Mieszany Korpus Lotniczy (MKL) – Composite Air Corps
Dywizja Lotnictwa Myśliwskiego (DLM) – Fighter Aviation Division
Dywizja Lotnictwa Myśliwskiego Obrony Powietrznej Kraju (DLM OPK) – Air Defence Fighter Aviation Division
Dywizja Lotnictwa Myśliwskiego Marynarki Wojennej (DLM MW) – Naval Fighter Aviation Division
Dywizja Lotnictwa Szturmowego (DLSz) – Attack Aviation Division
Pułk Lotnictwa Myśliwskiego (PLM) – Fighter Aviation Regiment
Pułk Lotnictwa Myśliwskiego Marynarki Wojennej (PLM MW) – Naval Fighter Aviation Regiment
Pułk Lotnictwa Myśliwsko-Bombowego (PLM-B) – Fighter-Bomber Aviation Regiment
Pułk Lotnictwa Szturmowego – Attack Aviation Regiment
Pułk Lotnictwa Szturmowego Marynarki Wojennej (PLSz MW) – Naval Attack Aviation Regiment
Pułk Lotnictwa Myśliwsko-Szturmowego (PLM-Sz) – Fighter-Attack Aviation Regiment
Pułk Lotnictwa Rozpoznawczego (PLR) – Reconnaissance Aviation Regiment
Pułk Lotnictwa Rozpoznania Taktycznego (PLR-T) – Tactical Reconnaissance Aviation Regiment
Pułk Lotnictwa Zwiadowczego (PLZ) – Reconnaissance Aviation Regiment
Samodzielny Pułk Lotnictwa Rozpoznawczego (SPLR) – Independent Reconnaissance Aviation Regiment
Pułk Lotnictwa Rozpoznania Taktycznego i Artyleryjskiego (PLRTiA) – Tactical Reconnaissance and Artillery Spotting Regiment
Pułk Szkolno-Treningowy Lotnictwa Myśliwskiego (PSz-T LM) Fighter Aviation Training Regiment
Pułk Szkolno-Bojowy (PSz-B) – Combat Training Regiment
Lotniczy Pułk Szkolno Bojowy – (LPSz-B) Air Combat Training Regiment
Oficerska Szkoła Lotnicza (OSL) – Officer Flying Training School
Lotnicza Eskadra Holownicza (LEH) – Target Tow Squadron

MiG-15

The MiG-15 was the first mass-produced Soviet turbojet-powered fighter of the second generation. Along with the US North American F-86 Sabre, first flown two months earlier, it was among the most advanced and successful fighter aircraft of the 1950s.

The turn of the 1940s and 1950s was a period of deteriorating international relationships between the East and West, and intense studies on turbojet engine development in the West. The first production aircraft with such powerplants saw combat as early 1944. These were German Messerschmitt Me 262 *Schwalbe*, Arado Ar 234 *Blitz*, Heinkel He 162 *Salamander* and British Gloster Meteor F Mk I. Studies on turbojet engine in the USSR were significantly delayed. The Soviets had no indigenous turbojet engine suitable as an aircraft powerplant. The technological advantage of the Western countries in aero-engine production was too great for the Soviet engine industry to overcome it. During 1945–46 engines designed by Alexander Mikulin and Arkhip Lyulka were only undergoing ground tests and were not suitable for use in production aircraft. The lack of capable and trusted turbojet engines made development of an aircraft with this prospective powerplant impossible. A partial solution to the lack of turbojet engins was possible thanks to well-developed war prize service in the Red Army (also known as famous "*trofyeynye otryady*"). It had great achievements in numerous fields. Even before the end of the war it captured German aircraft, such as Me 262, Ar 234 and He 162, powered by Junkers Jumo 109-004B and BMW 109-003A turbojet engines, and took them to the USSR. The service also supplied many of these engines. Some were damaged, but a large number of engines in working order was completed from them. They were handed over to design teams, which were tasked with developing turbojet-powered aircraft. *Trofyeynye otryady* had great achievements in the field of delivering to the USSR "widely understood" war prizes. Numerous aircraft designers were brought in, as well as documentation and prototypes of many turbojet- and rocket-powered designs. It was a great prize, enabling design teams to implement ready solutions for their own designs.

In the USSR the original idea of cloning and manufacturing the Me 262 aircraft was abandoned. However, on 2 April 1946 a decision to clone and manufacture BMW 003 and Junkers Jumo 004 engines was made, although these were unreliable designs with numerous flaws and poor development potenital. Nevertheless, they had one great advantage… they were available in the USSR. Production of Jumo 004B-1 engines, designated RD-10, was undertaken by Factory No. 26 in Ufa. The first batch of RD-10 engines had some German components and was plagued by numerous failures. The service life was limited to 25 hours. Factory No. 26 in Kazan undertook production of BMW 003 engines, designated RD-20. On 24 April 1946 the I-300 (F-1 or *izdeliye* F) aircraft, developed by OKB-155's Mikoyan and Gurevich design bureau, powered by two RD-20 engines, made its maiden flight. It later entered production as the MiG-9. Four hours later the second prototype of Yak-15, powered by an RD-10 engine took to the air. This aircraft also went into production.

Since the serial number of the aircraft was recorded in different ways in factory and military documents, the official version of the serial is used in the book, with the exception of photo captions where serials are recorded in the same way as they were painted on the airplanes.

1 *[1]: MiG-15 "6" of the 5.DLM OPL. Inside the digit 6 the serial number 38n2n55 is partially visible. Warsaw Bemowo Babice airfield, 1951.*

2

[2]: *MiG-15s "16" and "26" prior to take-off from Warsaw Bemowo Babice airfield.*

3

[3+4]: *MiG-15 aircraft of the 5. DLM OPL ready for inspection at Warsaw Bemowo Babice airfield. Among the delivered fighters were examples with tactical numbers in red, dark blue and yellow with dark blue or black outline. With these numbers they were operated in several Soviet fighter regiments, from which they were transferred. Therefore some numbers were repeated.*

4

[5+6]: MiG-15 fighters with tactical numbers "02" and "8" from the 1. PLM "Warszawa" *and "29" from the 13. PLM.*

Having at their disposal the German engines and their RD-10 and RD-20 clones, the design bureaus developed several jet-powered aircraft during 1946–1947. These were both prototypes of production aircraft and experimental fighters. On 13 November 1946 the Su-9 (*izdeliye* K), developed by the P. O. Sukhoi OKB-134 design bureau, first flew. It was powered by two RD-10 engines. It was similar in layout to the Me 262, but was not a copy. In 1946 the OKB-301 design bureau, led by S. A. Lavochkin, produced two aircraft, designated "150" and "152" which were built and flown. On 1 March 1947 the experimental "aircraft 156" with an RD-10F engine first flew. In June 1947 the "aircraft 160" (called "*stryelka*" – arrow) made its maiden flight. The "160" was the first aircraft in the USSR with swept wings. Powered by an RD-10F engine, it attained a speed of 1,050 km/h. In the Yakovlev 155 bureau the Yak-19 with RD-10F engine was developed. It was the first aircraft in the USSR to exceed the speed of 900 km/h. In its design the "step" fuselage layout, applied hitherto in the Yak-15/21 and Yak-17 aircraft family, was abandoned. In the Yak-19 the engine was mounted aft of the cockpit, with the exhaust nozzle at the end of the fuselage.

Apart from the new swept wing design, more capable engines with higher thrust and longer service lives were necessary to build a second generation fighter aircraft. There were still no such engines in the USSR. A trio of aviation experts (A. I. Mikoyan, V. I. Klimov and S. T. Kishkin), sent in late 1946 to Great Britain, managed to obtain clearance from Clement Attlee's Labour government for the purchase of advanced and economical Rolls-Royce turbojet engines. Rolls-Royce was the most experienced manufacturer of turbojet engines. The Nene Mk II engine of this series developed the highest thrust and had the reputation of being reliable. Even Josef Stalin himself initially did not believe in the success of this team's mission. However, this politically surprising deal was made! At this time the USSR was still seen as a wartime ally. The 180-hour service life of the British engines was a lot longer than that of the cloned German engines, amounting to mere 25 hours. The purchase contract was approved in the USSR on 11 March 1947. Thirty RR Derwent V, twenty RR Nene I and five RR Nene II engines were purchased. In Factory No. 500 the copy of the Derwent V engine was developed, therefore its designation was RD-500. The copy of the Nene I engine was made in Factory No. 45 and named RD-45 (RD stands for *Reaktivnyi Dvigatyel*, turbojet engine). Subsequently, unlicensed production of the cloned engines was launched. When the deliveries of the Rolls-Royce engines purchased in Great Britain began, the Derwent V engines were sent to the USSR first. The first ten Derwent V engines were shipped from Great Britain to Murmansk by sea on 21 March 1947. Second to arrive were the Nene I engines. In November 1947 15 Nene I engines were unloaded at Murmansk. After a series of fighters designed in the USSR on the basis of German engines and their copies, design of aircraft powered by the British engines began.

The first Soviet fighter powered by an English-supplied RR Derwent V engine, rated at 15.6 kN of thrust, was the Yak-23, developed in A. S. Yakovlev's OKB-115 design bureau and first flown on 8 July 1947. (The Yakovlev design bureau received seven Derwent V engines). The designers' demand for imported British engines was great, and obtaining them from the purchased lot was not easy. Rolls-Royce engines were also wanted by design teams developing jet-powered bomber aircraft. In the OKB-156 A. N. Tupolev was the first to use the Nene I engine in a bomber aircraft ("aircraft 77", Tu-12).

The purchase of new Rolls-Royce engines enabled the Soviets to embark on design of second generation fighter aircraft, attaining transonic speeds at high altitude, one hour endurance and heavily armed. For this purpose, on 11 March 1947 the Soviet Council of Ministers outlined the plan of development of experimental jet-powered aircraft in 1947. On this basis the Ministry of Aircraft Industry ordered Mikoyan's OKB-155 bureau to design a frontline fighter with pressurized cockpit and build two examples. An identical task to develop a front-line (tactical) fighter, powered by a RR Nene engine, was given to Lavochkin's OKB-301 bureau, while the Yakovlev bureau was tasked with developing a Derwent V-powered fighter. The Ministry specified the following tactical and technical requirements: maximum speed at ground level – 1,000 km/h, at 5,000 m – 1,020 km/h, climb to 5,000 m – 3.2 min, service ceiling – 13,000 m, maximum range at cruise speed at 5,000 m altitude – 1,200 km, take-off run – 700 m, landing run – 800 m, armament comprising one 45 mm and two 23 mm cannons, capability of carrying two 200 kg bombs instead of external fuel tanks. As early as 30 April Marshal K. A. Vyershynin, the Air Force commander-in-chief, approved the basic requirements, compliant to those specified by the ministry, with the exception of the 45 mm cannon, replaced by a 37 mm weapon.

On 30 December 1947 V. N. Yuganov made the maiden flight of the I-310 aircraft (factory designation S-1), designed by the team led by Artem Mikoyan, powered by a British RR Nene I engine (s/n 1036), rated at 20 kN of thrust. The second prototype, S-2, was fitted with the more powerful Nene II engine (s/n 1039), rated at 22.3 kN. It was flown by S. N. Anokhin on 27 May 1948. The third prototype, S-3, also powered by a genuine British Nene II engine, was a pre-production aircraft. It was first flown on 17 July 1948 by I. T. Ivashchenko.

The rival design bureaux, Lavochkin's OKB-301 and Yakovlev's OKB-115, embarked on development of transonic second generation fighter aircraft. Designing the swept-winged "aircraft 168" Semyon A. Lavochkin planned to equip it with a Nene II engine, generating higher thrust and 45 kg lighter than the Nene I. However, production of Nene II engines in Great Britain was slow and had not attained full capacity yet. Unexpectedly,

[7]: MiG-15 "08" from 2. Combat Training Squadron of No. 5 Officer Flying Training School at Radom-Sadków airfield.

7

[8]: MiG-15 "16" (s/n 1616). The number 1616 is visible in two places on the fuselage.

[9]: MiG-15 "26" from the 29. PLM based at Orneta.

deliveries of Nene engines to the USSR were halted for several months. There were concerns that deliveries of these engines might be cancelled for political reasons and the developing Cold War. Faced by the possibility that "aircraft 168" could not be fitted with a genuine RR Nene engine, it was first flown on 22 April 1948 with already produced clone of the Nene I engine, i.e. the RD-45. During tests in October 1948 the "aircraft 168" with two 23 mm and one 37 cannon attained a speed of 1,084 km/h (Ma 0,982) at an altitude of 2,750 m, climb to 5,000 m in two minutes, service ceiling of 14,570 m and range of 1,275 km. These performance figures showed that it was the best fighter aircraft in the USSR at that time. Having no chance to obtain a Nene II engine, Lavochkin developed the "aircraft 174" as a reserve design. It was a downsized variant of the "aircraft 168", with similar wing sweep of 37°20', powered by an available Derwent V engine. This engine was the lightest (565 kg), but also generated lower thrust in comparison with both Nene engines. Due to the lower thrust of this engine, the dimensions of "aircraft 168" were reduced (wingspan by 67 cm and length by 100 cm), to reduce its take-off weight to 3,600 kg. The weight of the armament was reduced by replacing the heavier 37 mm cannon with a third 23 mm cannon. A week after the maiden flight of Mikoyan's I-310 (S-1) prototype, Lavochkin's "174" first flew. This aircraft crashed four months later, on 11 May. Pilot Ivan Fyodorov survived. Soon the second example, designated "174D" (double) was completed and Fyodorov took it to the air on 12 June. During factory test flights "174D" attained a speed of 1,024 km/h at an altitude

[10]: MiG-15 "30" with characteristic shape of the digit "3" in the tactical number (s/n 1330?).

[11]: MiG-15 "32" of the 13 PLM.

of 8,000 m, climb to 5,000 m in 2,95 min, service ceiling of 14,600 m and range of 1,300 km. These were very good performance figures, taking into consideration the fact that the Derwent V engine, used out of necessity rather than choice, was the least powerful (15.9 kN) of the imported British engines.

State trials of the S-1, S-2 and "174D" prototypes by the NII WWS (Air Force Scientific and Research Institute) were conducted simultaneously. A wide test program encompassed performance figures and fuel consumption measurements, elaborate fatigue and tactical tests. The Lavochkin's prototype was a high wing aircraft, hence its landing gear retracted into fuselage side wells. Its short main landing gear wheel track made it prone to crosswinds on take-off and particularly on landing. It was a very unfavourable feature, especially during combat operations. In comparison with MiG-15 prototypes, the "174D" handled better in flight close to maximum speed. It was slightly lighter than the MiG-15. In contrast with the MiG-15, Lavochkin's aircraft had no design speed limitations. At maximum speed the "174D" had no tendency to self-induced descending turn or reverse reaction for rudder deflections. The MiG-15 had such flaws, which took a long time to eliminate. Lavochkin's aircraft featured lightweight and stiff wings, made using difficult and costly technology. It required metal block cutting, wing milling and using sophisticated wing-fuselage joints. Lavochkin's fighter was more agile than its rival. Mikoyan's prototype had better climb rate and heavier armament. The Council of Ministers decided to introduce into series production and service both the MiG-15 and the "174D" (factory designation *Izdeliye* 52). The "174D" soon received the military designation La-15.

In OKB-115, led by Yakovlev, three Yak-25 prototypes were built. The first prototype, powered by Derwent V engine, first flew on 2 November 1947. State evaluation of the prototypes was completed in September 1948. The Yak-25 was very agile, which was demonstrated at th Tushino air show, but did not go beyond the experimental fighter category. The subsequent Yak-30 fighter, a thorough modification of the previous type with 35-degree wing sweep, also powered by a Derwent V engine, first flew on 4 September 1948 and its factory trials continued until 16 December of that year. The aircraft was easy to fly even for an averagely skilled pilot, was very manoeuvrable and attained a speed of 1,025 km/h. State evaluation of the second, perfected, prototype designated Yak-30D (double) began at Saki (Crimea) as late as January 1949. By then the MiG-15 and La-15 fighter had been in production and the successful Yak-30 fighter arrived too late to enter production.

The S-1 and S-2 prototypes were not identical. The wings of the S-1 prototype were attached to the fuselage 8 cm further forward and had main spars and beams made of steel, while in the S-2 prototype these elements were made of aluminium alloy. The sliding canopy of the S-1 had an additional metal reinforcement of the glazing. The first two prototypes differed also in minor details in the main landing gear design. In the S-1 the retraction actuators were taken from the La-9 fighter. By 25 May 1948 both prototypes had in total made 51 flights (31 on the S-1 and 13 on the S-2). After this first stage of the trials it was concluded that the prototypes presented good flying and handling qualities. Therefore even before the completion of the trials the, on 15 March 1948, the Council of Ministers decided to put the aircraft, designated MiG-15, into production in Factory No.1 in Kuybyshev (now Samara). While the preparations of the assembly lines for MiG-15 production were going on, the S-1 and S-2 prototypes were sent for state trials to GK NII VVS (*Gosudarstvyennyi Krasnoznamyonnyi Nauchno-Ispytatyelnyi Institut Voyenno-Vozdushnykh Sil* – National, Red Banner Order-decorated Air Force Scientific and Research

12

13

[12]: MiG-15 "34" (s/n 1540) of the 13. PLM. Standing in the cockpit is flight instructor, 1st Lt Lucjan Sokólski.

[13]: MiG-15 "35" (s/n 20135) of the 11 PLM. In October 1951 it entered service in the 13. PLM.

[14]: MiG-15 "36" of the 62. PLM based at Poznań-Krzesiny, photographed during of two-ship formation flight to Wrocław. It is difficult to determine whether the aircraft is piloted by 1st Lt T. Krukowski or if he took photo of his wingman's aircraft.

14

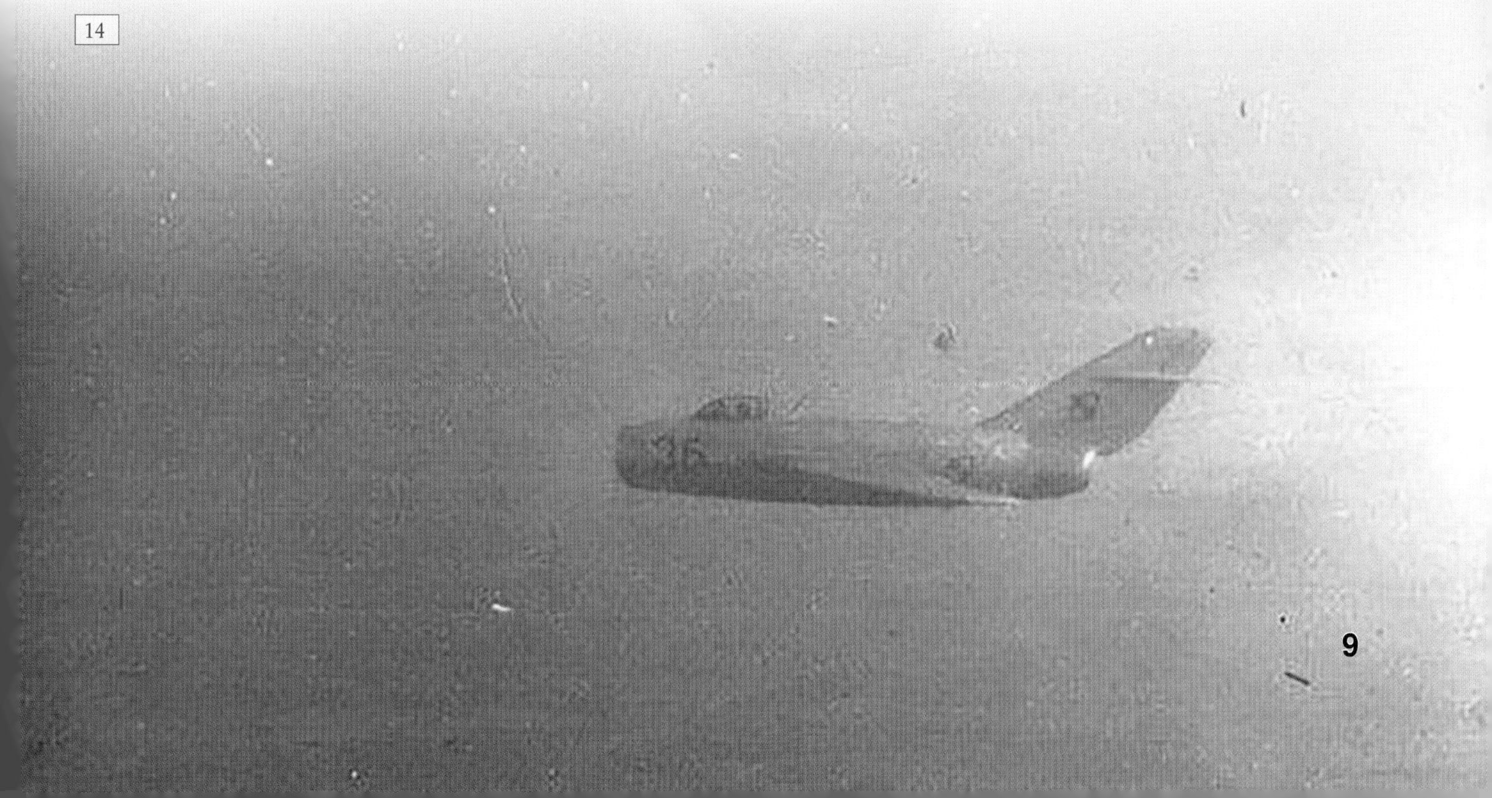

Institute) at Chkalovsk. The state evaluation was completed on 25 August 1948 and two days earlier, by decision No. 3210-1303 of the Council of Ministers, the MiG-15 was commissioned and put into mass production. By the same decision Lavochkin's "174D" aircraft, still undergoing state evaluation, was put into production.

Series production of the MiG-15 (*izdeliye* 50) aircraft was ordered in Factory No.1 in Kuybyshev, Factory No. 153 in Novosibirsk and Factory No. 381 in Moscow. Simultaneously, the Ministry of Aircraft Industry selected Factory No. 21 in Gorki (now Nizhny Novgorod) and Factory No. 292 for production of Lavochkin's "174D" fighter, now designated La-15. By a separate decision on 29 September 1948 the USSR Council of Ministers obliged the chief designer of OKB-155, A. I. Mikoyan, to introduce improvements in the S-3 prototype and send it for testing in November 1948. Further design changes were introduced in the S-3 prototype. A visible difference was the airbrakes, 0.48 sq.m. in area, mounted on the sides of the rear fuselage. The fuel system was redesigned and the capacity of the fuel tanks was increased from 1,340 l in the S-1 prototype to 1,460 l. Vertical stabilizer and aileron design was changed and emergency canopy jettison locks were added. On the cannon tray, lowered for ammunition loading, a place for an AFA-IM photo camera was made. Factory trials of the S-3 prototype were completed on 15 October 1948. The aircraft attained a speed of Ma 0.934. Test pilots, flying the S-3 reported cases of aircraft uncontrollability at maximum speed. At speeds exceeding 925 km/h the control stick became too heavy to move. Countering the intensifying rolling moment was beyond the pilot's physical strength. The necessary force to be used neared 18.5 kG. The aircraft had a tendency to go into a descending turn ("*valezhka*" in Russian). These unfavourable qualities prevented the aircraft from attaining maximum speed below 1,600 m. Evaluation of the S-3 prototype was conducted during 4 November – 3 December 1948 in the subsidiary of GK NII VVS at Saki in Crimea. In flights with g loads exceeding 7–7.6 g minor wing deformations occurred. Limitation of the maximum speed to Ma 0.92 or 1,067 km/h IAS was imposed. The trials revealed further flaws, that might have affected flying qualities and combat capability of the aircraft. The airbrakes needed improvements. To improve all-weather operation capability an instrument landing system was necessary and the accuracy of cannon fire also had to be improved.

After only one year from the maiden flight of the first prototype I-310 (S-1) the test pilot Viktor N. Yuganov took to the air the first production example of the MiG-15 aircraft, powered by the RD-45F, a copy of the RR Nene II.

For introduction of the next improvements the third production example of the MiG-15, serial number 101003, was selected. This aircraft received the designation RV. It received a number of modifications and improvements, which were responses to revealed design flaws. By the end of 1948, five production MiG-15 aircraft had been made in Kuybyshev. After the implementation of the required improvements, military evaluation of the MiG-15 aircraft commenced at Kubinka airfield near Moscow, in the 29th Fighter Aviation Regiment of the Guards based there. By 22 February 1949 the Kuybyshev facility delivered 15 examples from the first three production batches. The aircraft arrived by rail in crates. During a period of two months a sufficient number of pilots was trained and on 1 May 1949 the new fighters were demonstrated over the Red Square in Moscow. From 20 May – 15 September 1949

[15]: MiG-15 "5" in the Air Force Technical School (TSWL) at Zamość.

military tests of 20 MiG-15 aircraft from the 4th and 5th production batches were conducted. During these tests, there were four instances of flameout in level flight and in turns at an altitude exceeding 8,000 m. One of the tested aircraft did not make it to the airfield. It was damaged in a wheel-up landing and did not complete the tests. To prevent the engine flameout at high altitude, modifications in the fuel system were introduced. A system providing engine compressor bleed air to No. 1 fuel tank was added and an additional PNV-2 pump was installed. The PS-2 engine start-up panel was also installed. The modifications were introduced from the 6th production batch on.

On 22 June 1949 the representatives of GK NII VVS commenced control tests of the modified aircraft (s/n 1061017), which ended with success. Modifications and improvements implemented in this aircraft were recommended for introduction in series production aircraft. A couple of days earlier the MiG-15(SV) (s/n 101003), with further modifications and improvements, was again sent for control tests in GK NII VVS. Two NS-23 cannons were replaced with NR-23 cannons with higher rate of fire (850 rather than 550 rounds per minute). The ASP-1N gunsight was replaced with the newer ASP-3N. A B-5 hydraulic booster, making aileron control lighter, was added. Elevator aerodynamic balancing and engine restart system at altitudes below 5,000 m were improved. In total, 35 changes were introduced in (s/n 101003). They were gradually implemented in production aircraft. In 1949 the Kuybyshev factory built 510 MiG-15 aircraft. Along with the remaining factories, nos. 153 and 381, a total of 729 MiG-15 aircraft were built by the end of 1949. Production of MiG-15 aircraft in the USSR lasted only two years. After having built 1,344 MiG-15 aircraft in the fighter version, in early July 1950 series production of the improved MiG-15*bis* fighter began.

In Poland

The first aircraft from the Mikoyan and Gurevich design bureau arrived in Poland in 1951. At that time Yakovlev fighter aircraft were operated by the Polish air arm. The jet era in Polish aviation began with the introduction of the Yak-17V trainers and the first combat aircraft, the Yak-23 fighter. The Yak-17, tactical number "29", was the first jet aircraft with Polish markings which appeared in Polish skies on 20 August 1950. It was one of three Yak-17 jets purchased. The flight demonstration of this aircraft became a symbolic entry of Polish aviation into the jet era. However, the role of the Yak-17 in Poland was limited to familiarization flights and demonstration of the fighter with a new type of engine.

The first MiGs that arrived in Poland were two-seat UTI MiG-15 trainers. On 6 July 1951 four such aircraft (s/nos 10411, 10423, 10424 and 10425), landed at Warsaw Bemowo airfield. They were flown by Soviet instructors, assigned to train the Polish aircrews. The aircraft entered the inventory of the 1. PLM "*Warszawa*". Nearly two weeks later, on 19 July 1951, the first MiG-15 aircraft landed at Bemowo airfield. They were transferred from a Soviet unit based in East Germany near Berlin. These aircraft (s/nos 0227, 0231, 0234, 0236, 0245, 0249 and 1323), were built in 1949.

They were the first MiG-15 fighters that the entered inventory of the 1. PLM "*Warszawa*" *(Pułk Lotnictwa Myśliwskiego* – Fighter Aviatin Regiment). The first public demonstration took place on 22 July 1951 during an air parade over Bank Square in Warsaw. Five MiG-15s, led by Lt Col. Jan Frey-Bielecki, assisted

[16]: MiG-15 "38" in the Air Force Technical School (TSWL) at Zamość.

[17+18]: MiG-15 "39" (s/n 119174) as trainer aircraft in the 59. PSz-B at Biała Podlaska.

by four MiG-15s piloted by Soviet instructors, flew in column with five three-ship Yak-23 flights. In August formation of another regiment within the 5. DLM (*Dywizja Lotnictwa Myśliwskiego* – Fighter Aviation Division) commenced at Warsaw-Bemowo (Babice) airfield. On 9 August 1951 the newly-formed 13. PLM took over 13 Yak-23 fighters from the 1. PLM. A further seven Yak-23s were transferred to the 13. PLM from the staff flight of the 5. DLM. In August and September the 13. PLM received two Yak-17V trainers, one from the 1. PLM and the other from the 2. PLM. On the Aviation Day, 23 August 1951, a MiG-15 flown by Maj. Stanisław Łozowski was demonstrated.

The MiG-15 fighters, delivered from the USSR in July and October 1951, were initially assigned to two regiments, the 1. PLM and 13. PLM, which received 30 aircraft each. The 1. PLM received aircraft with serial numbers: 0141, 0227, 0228, 0230, 0231, 0233, 0234, 0236, 0237, 0245, 0249, 0395, 0306, 0307, 0308, 0310, 1238, 1307, 1308, 1310, 1238, 1307, 1316, 1317, 1319, 1321, 1324, 1325, 1328, 1330, 1338, 1340, 1704 and 2055. The 13. PLM received the following aircraft: 0100, 0102, 0104, 0132, 0133, 0137, 0140, 0142, 0146, 0149, 0201, 0303, 0507, 1123, 1214, 1226, 1302, 1329, 1335, 1423, 1429, 1522, 1540, 1616, 8038, 9013, 20076, 20135, 20136 and 20144. Aircraft (s/n 20100) was intended for the staff flight of the 5. DLM. They were not brand new aircraft, as the factories in the USSR had ceased their production a year earlier. These aircraft, transferred from Soviet fighter regiments, were in varying technical condition. The oldest were 51 aircraft built in 1949, among them aircraft built by Factory No. 381 in Moscow. The

Moscow-built MiG-15s assigned to the 1. PLM had the following serial numbers: 0227, 0228, 0230, 0231, 0233, 0234, 0236, 0237, 0245 and 0249. For instance, full serial number of the first of the aforementioned Moscow-built aircraft was 3810227. In this number 381 was the number of the Moscow facility, 02 was the number of the production batch and 27 was the number of the example within the production batch. The newest MiG-15 aircraft delivered to Poland were built in April and May 1950. They were from the last, 20th production batch built by the Kuybyshev facility. They had the following serial numbers: 120076, 120135, 120136 i 120144. To the 20th production batch from the Kuybyshev facility also belonged the 100th example, i.e. MiG-15 serial number 120100, which was assigned to the staff flight of the 5. DLM. The last of this batch, s/n 120144, was also the last MiG-15 built in Kuybyshev Factory No. 1. Serial numbers of the MiG-15s built in Kuybyshev started with 1 – the number of the factory. For instance, in aircraft number 120144, after 1, denoting number of the factory, the number of the production batch – 20 – was placed, followed by the number of individual aircraft within the batch, here – 144. In 1951 the USSR delivered to Poland a total of 61 used MiG-15 fighters. Moreover, in 1952 the only new example of this type was delivered from Kuybyshev to Poland. It was sent to the WSK Mielec factory as a "production pattern" before commencement of the Lim-1 licence fighters production. In spite of appearances, this aircraft was not a pattern example for the entire batch of Lim-1 fighters. It served only to master the technology of assembly of the license aircraft. The MiG-15 (s/n 119074) was entered into 1. PLM inventory on 30 September 1952.

In Polish writing we encounter two instances of the same MiG-15 aircraft having two different serial numbers, or even these numbers are written together. Probably this situation occurred because different records of number of the same example appeared in various documents. The first such instance concerns the aforementioned MiG-15 (s/n 119074). The number 113074 is also erroneously attributed to this aircraft and in other versions of the numeration of this aircraft these two numbers are mentioned together. It was delivered to Mielec before commencement of production of Lim-1 license fighters. Erroneously described as the "pattern" aircraft, this was the newest MiG-15 built by the Kuybyshev facility in 1951. It differed from the aircraft of earlier production batches in the introduced modifications. They were the results of prior service of the MiG-15s in combat units. It had more complex equipment and different layout of instruments in the cockpit. It differed from earlier examples in modifications of the electrical system and improved cockpit heating system. All these improvements were implemented in aircraft of the 19th rather than the 13th production batch, as the erroneously mentioned number 113074 may suggest.

A similar situation occurred with MiG-15 (s/n 12055) which, introduced in the inventory of the 1. PLM, from the beginning of its service, flew in the staff flight of the 5. DLM at Bemowo airfield. In Polish texts this aircraft is described as having two numbers simultaneously, 2055/20055, in other publications this latter number was attributed to it separately. This aircraft was built in the Kuybyshev facility on 27 October 1949 within the 12th production batch. Therefore it could not have received the number 20055, as aircraft with similar numbers left the Kuybyshev facility about half a year later. Therefore the proper number is 2055 and the full number is 112055.

In January 1952 formation of the third unit within the 5. DLM began. It was the 31. PLM, initially equipped with Yak-23 aircraft. The decision of Air Force Headquarters stipu-

[19]: MiG-15 "24" on display in front of the Palace of Culture in Warsaw on 30 September 1961.

lated equipping the entire 5. DLM with MiG-15 fighters, while the 7. DLM was to be equipped with Yak-23 aircraft. All Yak-23 and Yak-17V aircraft on strength with the 5. DLM were transferred to the 7. DLM. On 10 January another rotation of MiG-15 fighters began.

To equip a new regiment with this type of fighter, there was a need to transfer several aircraft from other units. Ten MiG-15s were transferred to the 31. PLM from each of the 1. PLM and 13. PLM. The 31. PLM gave previously operated Yak-23s to the disposal of the 7. DLM. From then on each of three regiments of the 5. DLM based at Bemowo airfield had on strength about 20 modern MiG-15 fighters each, rather than the mandatory 30. This number of MiG-15s on strength of the 5. DLM did not last long. In May 1952 another regiment began to be equipped with MiG-15s. It was the 41. PLM based at Malbork, part of the 9. DLM. It received 14 MiG-15 fighters transferred from three regiments. Three were transferred from the 1. PLM, a further five from the 13. PLM and six from the 31. PLM. The MiG-15 was the first combat aircraft operated by the 41. PLM.

In August 1952 formation of the 10. DLM began. Again the 5. DLM was forced to reduce its inventory and transfer another batch of 10 MiG-15 aircraft, taken from the Division's three regiments, to the Słupsk-based 28. PLM.

On 11 April 1952 a crash in the 1. PLM took place. The MiG-15 tactical number "17", serial number 1325, crashed near Nowiny, 27 km from Bemowo airfield, killing the pilot, W/O Ryszard Apalkow. Another crash took place in the 1. PLM the next month, on 31 May 1952. The pilot, W/O Tadeusz Polek, who took off in the MiG-15 tactical number "26" (s/n 0233), on a training sortie to practice advanced flying skills, was killed. The aircraft crashed near Wiązowna.[1]

To be able to fulfil the monthly plan of Lim-1 aircraft production, it was decided in WSK Mielec to deliver the genuine MiG-15 (s/n 119074), to the Air Force. It entered the inventory of the 1. PLM on 30 September 1952 (findings made by Grzegorz Klimasiński on the basis of source materials). This aircraft was delivered to the WSK Mielec to master the technology of assembly. It cannot be named "production pattern", as many of its details differed from the technical documentation supplied to the WSK factory. Original documentation of that time denies it.

1 Chronology and some facts concerning crashes of Polish fighter aircraft during 1952–1960 is given among others after a joint study, edited by Lt Col. Dr Józef Zieliński, "*Pamięci lotników wojskowych* 1945–2003". Many pieces of information are from Grzegorz Klimasiński's archive.

[20]: A MiG-15 as a technical aid in the Air Force Technical School (TSWL) at Zamość. The tactical number "29" and serial number 0507 are visible on the exhaust nozzle cover.

[21]: MiG-15 "29" (s/n 0507) in the Air Force Technical School (TSWL) at Zamość, 1950s.

MiG-15 fighters delivered to Poland (shortened serial numbers): 0100**, 0102**, 0104*, 0132, 0133, 0137, 0140, 0141, 0142, 0146, 0149, 0201, 0227, 0228, 0230, 0231, 0233, 0234, 0236, 0237, 0245, 0249, 0303, 0305, 0306, 0307, 0308, 0310, 0507**, 1123*, 1214, 1226, 1238, 1302, 1307, 1316, 1317, 1319, 1321, 1324, 1325, 1328, 1329, 1330, 1335, 1338, 1340, 1423, 1429, 1522, 1540, 1616, 1704, 8038, 9013, 2055, 20076*, 20100*, 20135*, 20136*, 20144*, 119074**.

* *Examples built in 1950*

** *Examples built in 1951*

The remaining examples were built in 1949.

The situation with equipment in regiments operating MiG-15 fighters and awaiting deliveries of new Lim-1 fighters was getting complicated. The TBO (time between overhauls) of many MiG-15 aircraft were due to end in 1953. Major overhauls of 53 MiG-15 aircraft were necessary. Start up of MiG-15 aircraft production was difficult. During September – December 1952 assembly of the license aircraft virtually stopped. It was caused by failure in mastering wing assembly and poor quality of the flaps and ailerons produced. By the end of December 1952 only two aircraft had been assembled. In January 1953 the situation was not much better. Only two aircraft were flown and delivered to the Air Force. Examples which had been being assembled since December were being completed.

The 26. PLM, formed at Królewo Malborskie airfield, was detached from the 9. DLM and along with the 40. PLM was attached to the 11. DLM. On 10 October 1953 it was moved to a new airfield at Zegrze Pomorskie. The regiment, which in July 1953 had had in its inventory 12 Yak-23 fighters since 24 May 1952, received 13 MiG-15 fighters on 31 October 1953.

In the autumn of 1953 the 3. PLM received 21 MiG-15 aircraft. Previously operated Yak-23s were transferred to the 21. PLZ (*Pułk Lotnictwa Zwiadowczego* – Reconnaissance Aviation Regiment), based at Poznań-Ławica airfield and to a new training squadron being formed at OSL-5 (*Oficerska Szkoła Lotnicza nr 5* – No. 5 Officer Flying Training School) in Radom.

Re-equipping of the Słupsk-based 28. PLM and Malbork-based 41. PLM with more advanced MiG-15bis fighters in January 1953 allowed for transferring previously operated MiG-15s to regiments until then operating the Yak-23. Nine MiG-15s were transferred from the 28. PLM to the 25. PLM, also based at Słupsk. The first four MiG-15s with tactical numbers: "23" (s/n 0137), "7" (s/n 0201), "28" (s/n 1226) and "27" (s/n 1616) were delivered to the 25. PLM on 24 December 1952.

One of the first MiG-15 aircraft delivered to the 25. PLM, serial number 1226, tactical number "28", was lost in a crash on 5 February 1953. On take-off from Słupsk the pilot rotated and lifted off too soon. The aircraft, losing speed, lost stability, banked to the left, crashed and caught fire. The aircraft caught and the pilot, 1st Lt Zdzisław Karaszewski, was killed. In February all previously operated Yak-23 fighters were withdrawn from the 25. PLM. On the last day of February 1953 the 25. PLM accepted a second batch of five MiG-15 fighters from the 28. PLM, with tactical "26" (s/n 0132), "28" (s/n 0141), "6" (s/n 0142), "11" (s/n 1522) and "21" (s/n 20135). The aircraft "28" (s/n 0141), received in the second batch in late February, was damaged on 18 May 1953 in a wheels-up landing at Redzikowo airfield. The pilot, 2nd Lt Mieczysław Sroka, had no injuries and the aircraft was repaired and returned to service.

On 12 June 1953 there was a crash in the 28. PLM, in which two aircraft were lost and two pilots killed. A squadron of MiG-15s took off from Redzikowo airfield in two-ship flights arranged in echelon right formation to practice coordination in combat formations. Over the village of Damnica, at an altitude of 600 m, the aircraft piloted by 2nd Lt Zdzisław Kaniak collided with another one, piloted by 2nd Lt Franciszek Barzyński. 2nd Lt Kaniak ejected at 150 m. The parachute had not enough time to deploy and the pilot was killed, as was 2nd Lt Barzyński.

The 41. PLM transferred its 14 MiG-15s to the 29. PLM, based at Orneta. The Polish coast was then protected by modern MiG-15bis fighters from Słupsk-based 28. PLM and Malbork-based 41. PLM and by older MiG-15s from Słupsk-based 25. PLM and Orneta-based 29. PLM. In August 1953 the 25. PLM was moved from Słupsk to Pruszcz Gdański air base.

In 1954 in the Polish air arm there were four crashes, in which five pilots and seven MiG-15 aircraft were lost. The first

22

[22]: MiG-15 "24" (s/n 0308) is the aircraft of Capt. Andrzej Dobrzeniecki from Krzesiny-based 62. PszT LM on display at the Citadel in Poznań, probably in 1955. The Monument of Heroes is visible in the background.

[23]: MiG-15 "100" (s/n 120100) from the staff flight of 5.DLM OPL headquarters, towed by a Dodge WC-51 truck at Warsaw Bemowo/Babice airfield.

23

of these crashes took place in the 26. PLM, based at Zegrze Pomorskie. On 4 March 1954 2d Lt Jerzy Golik was flying a MiG-15 in a two-ship flight at low altitude. Making a turn, the flight flew into clouds. The pilot deployed airbrakes, causing loss of speed and a stall. The aircraft crashed near the village of Kliszno, district Koszalin. 2nd Lt Golik was killed.

On 27 April 1954 Malbork-based 41. PLM lost two MiG-15 aircraft and two pilots in a crash. On that day the pilots were tasked with a close formation sortie to practice typical two-ship formation attacks at an altitude of 2,300 m. The wingman's (W/O Zbigniew Klimkiewicz) aircraft hit the leader's (2nd Lt Adam Zabawa) aircraft with the tailplane. The leader's aircraft lost a wing, went out of control, crashed and burned. The pilot was killed. W/O Klimkiewicz's aircraft with damaged tailplane went into an uncontrolled dive and hit the ground in inverted flight. The pilot ejected, but was also killed because the parachute failed to open due to too low altitude. The crash took place near Wielkie Walichnowy.

On 22 May 1954 sorties to practice combat two-ship formation flying in fair weather conditions at the altitude of 9,000 m were scheduled in Słupsk-based 28. PLM. 1st Lt Franciszek Szczyglak was flying a MiG-15. Executing a turn at an altitude of 800 m the aircraft went into dive for unknown reasons and crashed between Korlino and Królewo near Sławno. The pilot did not eject and was killed.

Another crash in the 26. PLM in 1954 occurred on 9 September at Zegrze Pomorskie. On that day the pilots practised formation flights in MiG-15 aircraft. During the assembly of eight aircraft 1st Lt Mieczysław Kochanowski, joining the formation, flew under the airplane piloted by 2nd Lt Jerzy Świeńczak. He hit the underside of 2nd Lt Świeńczak's airplane with his vertical stabilizer, losing control over his own aircraft. He ejected successfully about 10 km away from base. Trying to save the aircraft, 2nd Lt Świeńczak attempted to land his damaged aircraft at the home base, but did not succeed and was killed. In one day the 26. PLM lost two MiG-15 aircraft and one pilot.

The year 1954 was marked by a MiG-15 crash also in the history of Świdwin-based 40. PLM. It occurred on 17 August 1954 during a two-ship formation flight. Flying as the wingman, 1st Lt Stanisław Harmata lost the lead aircraft from sight and lost spatial orientation. He continued flying in severe weather conditions at night. Seeing lights on the ground he decided not to eject, but to make an emergency off-airport landing. The aircraft crashed in East Germany near Gelen, 35 km away from Frankfurt am Oder and the pilot was killed.

Soon after the takeover of fighter pilot training by Radom-based OSL-5 the concept of forming a training regiment emerged. The inefficiency of the training system was getting increasingly exposed. It resulted from increased recruitment of officer cadets, first trained theoretically at Dęblin-based OSL-4 The training at Dęblin was shortened in accordance with the rule "teach only what is needed during the war". The graduates of the Radom school graduated with little flying time on piston-powered aircraft. They had no experience in flying jets. There were attempts to make up for these shortages by training the fresh pilots in training squadrons of the combat

[24]: MiG-15 "10", from the 5. DLM at Warsaw Bemowo/Babice airfield. Seven-digit s/n 381xxxx on the right nosewheel door indicates that the aircraft was produced by Factory No. 381 in Moscow.

regiments. However, this supplemental training often evolved into training ab initio. Forming of the training squadron was postponed due to lack of a qualified instructor cadre and proper number of jet aircraft. A provisional attempt to improve the situation was to assign training duties to the 11. PLM OPL (*Pułk Lotnictwa Myśliwskiego Obrony Przeciwlotniczej* Air Defence Fighter Aviation Regiment), formed in December 1950 at Ławica airfield in Poznań, moved to Krzesiny in April 1952. From December 1952 the 11. PLM trained pilots from other fighter units at Krzesiny air base in Yak-23 aircraft, with which it was equipped from February 1953. By 30 April the last pistion-powered Yak-9P fighters in the inventory were written off. On 1 October the 11. PLM had 17 Yak-23 aircraft in its inventory. Only in accordance with the plan of forming a fighter training unit at Krzesiny air base in August 1954 did the first MiG-15 aircraft arrive. Twelve MiG-15 aircraft were assigned to two squadrons of the 11. PLM. The 1st Squadron operated aircraft with the following serial numbers: 0230, 0231, 0249, 1238, 1307 and 1522. The 2nd Squadron was equipped with the following aircraft: s/nos 0228, 0236, 0303, 0305, 20076 and 20135. By the September 1954 order of the Ministry of Defence formation of the new, two-squadron 62 PSz-T LM (Pułk Szkolno-Treningowy Lotnictwa Myśliwskiego – Fighter Aviation Training Squadron) began on the basis of Krzesiny-based 11. PLM, subordinated to the 6. DLM OPK (Dywizja Lotnictwa Mysliwskiego Obrony Powietrznej Kraju – Air Defence Fighter Aviation Division). The new regiment was to take over the task of training pilots in jet fighters from the 11. PLM. In the early period of 62. PSz-T LM operations the groundcrews of both squadrons were also trained for a month. Technical test flights and sorties limited to maintain proficiency among reduced aircrew cadre were sporadically flown. During 25–26 October the 3rd Squadron of the 11. PLM (equipped with 10 brand new Lim-1 aircraft) was moved to Debrzno air base. Since then only the 62. PSz-T LM was stationed at Krzesiny air base. Near the end of the second training tour, scheduled for March-June 1955, two MiG-15 aircraft collided in the air during a two-ship formation flight. The wingman's aircraft, flown by the trainee 2nd Lt Skrzypczak, hit the lead aircraft, flown by 1st Lt Zbigniew Możdżeń with the left wing, damaging the lead aircraft's right wing, breaking the windshield and jamming the canopy, making ejection impossible. Fortunately, 1st Lt Możdżeń did not lose control over the damaged aircraft and made a wheels-up emergency landing on the grass part of the airfield, sustaining minor injuries. The wingman also landed his slightly damaged aircraft safely.

Intense training in the 62. PSz-T LM and large number of sorties flown caused the service life of the unit's aircraft to expire quickly. The inventory was provisionally complemented with MiG-15 aircraft obtained from other fighter regiments – mainly from Malbork-based 41. PLM and Łęczyca-based 13. PLM. The aicraft's service at Krzesiny was nearing end and a few MiG-15s remained in service in this regiment until October 1955.

During the riots of June 1956 in Poznań the command post, from which the pacification of Poznań was controlled, was located at Ławica airfield. The forces were commanded by Stanisław Popławski, a Soviet Army general in Polish uniform. The account of these memorable June days, written by Major Józef Mizera, the then aerial gunnery chief of Malbork-based 9. DLM, is interesting. By the order of Brig. Gen. Jan Frey-Bielecki, Maj. Mizera flew a reconnaissance sortie to scout the movements of the Soviet Army forces. He recalled:

"*During one of the last days of June I was a duty officer at the command post of the 9. DLM. About 8 o'clock a Lim-2 appeared at the altitude of about 200 m over Malbork air base. Who is above me? – I asked, giving my call sign – Is the runway checked, am I cleared to land? – was the answer without a call sign. However, I recognized the characteristic voice of General Frey-Bielecki. - I've checked the runway, you are cleared to land. When General's Lim was rolling on the runway, I drove the staff car to meet the unexpected guest. I reported myself as the division's duty officer. I knew that you were on duty today – said the general, offering his hand. Now get to the point, time is running out. Please order to prepare my aircraft to fly again. The Air Traffic Duty officer shall not report my arrival and departure. Please order to prepare a MiG-15 equipped with a photo camera (AFA-BA-40), you will fly a reconnaissance mission. Set the camera for photos from 300 m altitude. You will personally notify the commander of the 10. DLM at Słupsk, Col. Stanisław Tanana that I am at your base and I'm flying on in a moment. What could I say? Yes, sir. When we arrived at the airport, he showed me the target area on the map. It was the zone Elbląg – Frombork – Braniewo – Pieniężno. Upon completion of the mission you will land at Orneta airfield, I'll be waiting for you there. And the most important thing – I am interesting in troop movements on the roads from Kaliningrad and stopping places of larger troop assemblies. Upon completion of this mission you will land at Orneta, as I have said, I'll be waiting for you there. Please maintain absolute radio silence during the entire mission – he added. When the maps were prepared and the aircraft ready, we climbed into the cockpits. He embarked in his Lim-2, I boarded the MiG-15. I took off before 9 o'clock. After the take-off, at low altitude I headed for Elbląg and farther into the target area, maintaining radio silence as ordered. On the way, mainly in the area of Braniewo, I noticed armoured columns, fuel bowsers and other vehicles, heading south-west from Kaliningrad. Some vehicles were moving, other stood on dirt roads and forest clearings. Within 15 minutes I photographed all I could in several runs. When the film (18x2,800 cm) ran out, I switched the camera off and headed for Orneta airfield at low altitude. Being close to it, I descended to minimum altitude to avoid being detected by radar. On the taxiway I spotted the general's airplane heading towards the flightline and I headed there as well after landing. When I turned the engine off, the general was waiting at my wing. – Was there anything to photograph? – he asked. There was plenty – I answered. Thank you. After refuelling you will head for Malbork and I – to your knowledge – to Krzesiny off Poznań, events of highest importance are going on there. The film case from my camera was placed in the general's aircraft and I showed him the reconnaissance area on the map. I took off second from Orneta and after 10 minutes I was back in Malbork.*"

The account of Col. Józef Mizera is also interesting because of the MiG-15 being fitted with an AFA-BA-40 camera at the disposal of Malbork-based 9. DLM.

On 17 May 1955 there was a fatal crash at OSL-5 in Radom. Officer Cadet Henryk Chmielewski of the 1st Training

Squadron was flying his second circuit pattern solo sortie in a MiG-15. Poorly trained pilot bounced the aircraft on touchdown. Trying to correct the error the pilot bounced the aircraft twice and after the third one turned the aircraft wheels up and hit the runway with the nose. The aircraft burned with the pilot.

On 30 May 1956 the third crash of a MiG-15 in the 26. PLM, based at Zegrze Pomorskie took place. 2nd Lt Henryk Tokarski took off in a two-ship formation to attack the lead aircraft at an altitude of 6,000 m. He entered a spin and was not able to recover. The aircraft crashed near Wyszewo, district Koszalin The regiment lost its third pilot and fourth MiG-15 aircraft.

The 39. PLM, formed in 1951 at Cracow-Czyżyny airfield, was moved to the ultimate base at Mierzęcice in May 1952. At Mierzęcice the regiment, equipped with Yak-23 aircraft, received the first MiG-15 fighters and UTIMiG-15 combat trainers in May 1952.

The MiG-15 jet fighters were also introduced for training at OSL-4 at Dęblin. Thus both Officer Flying Training Schools converted to train pilots in jet aircraft. It happened first in the Radom school during 1952–1953. Conversion to MiG-15 jet fighters in training was described in the Scientific Notes by Col. Andrzej Majewski in 2004. He enclosed an interesting piece of information in this description: "*In October 1956 we ferried the first MiG-15 fighters of the disbanded 5. DLM (1., 13., and 31. PLM) from Warsaw – Bemowo/Babice airfield to Dęblin. These were of the old variant, so-called "pushbuttons", with Siemens pushbutton switches*". (In later MiG-15bis the circuit breakers were in the form of rows of toggle switches on two panels on the port and starboard side of the cockpit). The complete transition to pilot training on jet aircraft in the Dęblin school took place during 1955–1957.

In September 1952 the first Lim-1 fighters, license built in Poland, began to enter service. Simultaneously the MiG-15s were gradually transferred to attack units to replace piston-powered Il-10 aircraft. It was an interim solution, intended for the period of development and production startup of an attack aircraft in Poland. At Bydgoszcz airfield a provisional training centre was established, converting pilots of piston-powered Il-10 attack aircraft to MiG-15 jet fighters. During 1956–1960 aircrews of the regiments of the 8. and 16. DLSz (*Dywizja Lotnictwa Szturmowego* – Attack Aviation Division) were converted to jets. The last to convert to MiG-15s was the 53. PLSz (*Pułk Lotnictwa Szturmowego* – Attack Aviation Regiment), based at Mirosławiec. A large number of MiG-15 aircraft were transferred from fighter regiments to the 51. PLM-Sz (*Pułk Lotnictwa Myśliwsko-Szturmowego* – Fighter-Attack Aviation Regiment), based at Piła.

Next the MiG-15s were transferred to air combat training regiments of both Officer Flying Training Schools. The MiG-15, S-102 and Lim-1 fighters were transferred to three combat training regiments, formed from 1958 on. These were: 58. LPSz-B (*Lotniczy Pułk Szkolno-Bojowy* – Air Combat Training Regiment) based at Dęblin, 59. LPSz-B based at Biała Podlaska and 61. LPSz-B based at Nowe Miasto nad Pilicą (both regiments were subordinated to OSL-5 in Radom).

Fourteen MiG-15 aircraft were lost in crashes during the type's service in Poland.

[25]: MiG-15 (s/n 1302), with three-digit tactical number "302". It was first operated by the 13. PLM. At that time it probably had a two-digit tactical number.

26 *[26]: MiG-15 of the 1. PLM in natural metal finish, covered with transparent lacquer coating, with red tactical number "4", black serial number 0310 ahead of it and small-capacity expended cartridge case container for the NR-23 cannons.*

27 *[27]: MiG-15 "4" (s/n 0310) of the 1. PLM, Warsaw Bemowo/Babice airfield, 1951.*

28

[28]: MiG-15 of the 13. PLM, tactical number "38" with characteristic shape of the digit "8", covered with aluminium enamel paint after overhaul.

29

[29]: MiG-15 tactical number "38", operated by the 13. PLM. It probably has s/n 0308.

MiG-15bis

Development of a new version of the fighter resulted from the development of an improved copy of the Rolls-Royce Nene Mk II engine in the OKB-117 design bureau, led by Vladimir I. Klimov. The efficiency of the compressor was improved by 20%. The thrust of the RD-45F engine was improved by 12%, from 22.26 kN to 26.5 kN. The engine, designated VK-1, had a 100-hour time between overhauls (TBO). In May 1949 a decision to put the engine into production was made. With a better engine, the OKB-155 embarked on further modifications of the MiG-15. In the Soviet Air Force a division of second generation fighters was made, to promising and unpromising.

To the former the MiG-15 was included, to the latter the La-15, powered by the RD-500 engine which was not intended for further development. On the grounds of economy and materiel supply problem it was decided to limit the number of fighter aircraft types in service. It was patterned on the similar, then implemented, concept of "the only tactical bomber aircraft type", which was the Il-28. The production version of this bomber was also powered by VK-1 engines. The decision of the Soviet Government on 14 May 1949 stipulated series production of the MiG-15, which was to be the only tactical fighter aircraft type of the Soviet Air Force. The factories producing Yak-23 and La-15 fighters were obliged to terminate their production and convert to MiG-15 production with the VK-1 engine from June 1950. V. K. Klimov was obliged to ultimately increase the TBO of the VK-1 engine to 250 hours within a year, in the first stage to 200 hours. The prototype of the MiG-15bis was based on the production MiG-15, serial number 105015. The RD-45F engine was replaced by a VK-1. It required changes in the rear section of the fuselage, because the VK-1 engine had a longer exhaust nozzle and was of larger diameter than the RD-45F. The BS-1 hydraulic amplifier was also installed. The air brakes were enlarged to improve their efficiency. To reduce the nose pitching moment after their deployment, their rotation axis was shifted 22 degrees from the vertical. The installation of the VK-1 engine resulted in reduction of No. 1 fuel tank capacity by 60 l and change of position of several engine and equipment access hatches.

The lower fuel tank capacity reduced the range by 180 km. Minor changes were also made to the forward fuselage section. The barrels of NR-23 cannons were placed closer to the aircraft's longitudinal axis, which improved accuracy. The modified MiG-15 s/n 105015 was designated MiG-15bis and received factory designations SD, *izdeliye* 53 (product 53). Initially it was also briefly referred to as the MiG-17. After factory trials it was sent for state evaluation at GK NII VVS. After six days of testing, compressor stall and high-frequency engine vibration occurred in flight above 8,000 m. The testing was halted and

[30]: MiG-15bis "346" (s/n 133046) after being hijacked by 1st Lt Franciszek Jarecki from Słupsk-based 28. PLM and landing at Rønne airfield, Bornholm, on 5 March 1953.

30

[31]: MiG-15bis "376" (s/n 133076). Its first combat unit was the 28. PLM. After the escape of the second MiG-15bis to Bornholm it was transferred from Słupsk to the 31. PLM.

the aircraft was sent back to the design bureau for correction of the defects. A new VK-1 engine (s/n 94-29), was installed and on 21 October the SD aircraft was again sent to GK NII VVS. Unfortunately, the high-frequency engine vibration and compressor stall occurred again. After 38 flights the deputy commander of the VVS ordered a halt to the state evaluation, on 15 January 1950. After the agreement of the chief designer with the commander of the VVS the third VK-1 engine (s/n 94-104), which had undergone several modifications to eliminate compressor stalls, was installed. The armament was also improved in the SD aircraft and the armament testing was added to the evaluation program, resumed on 3 February. However, on 15 March, after 16 flights the trials had to be halted again. The cause was the same – engine vibration and compressor stalls, as with the previous engine. A new VK-1 engine (s/n F-0143) was installed in the SD aircraft for the fourth time and on 18 March flight testing resumed. The aircraft flew 35 sorties. It was ignored that the defects identified previously still persisted, although to a lesser extent and it was deemed that the SD aircraft completed this ill-fated stage of trials. The testing revealed that, in comparison with production RD-45F – powered MiG-15s, the introduction of the VK-1 engine and other modifications significantly improved virtually all of the aircraft's characteristics. The performance improved, apart from the range, reduced by 180 km. The diminished range resulted from smaller capacity of the No.1 fuel tank and increased fuel consumption by the new engine. The maximum speed attained by the SD aircraft (MiG-15bis s/n 105015) with VK-1 engine (s/n 94-29) was 1,076 km/h. Controllability along all three axes improved. All controls became lighter, also after deployment of the airbrakes. Although the controls were heavy beyond an acceptable norm, according to pilots they were satisfactory. Still unsolved was the tendency to go into a descending turn ("*valezhka*"). The pilots were particularly disappointed with the system of VK-1 engine turbine RPM adjustment, not permitting normal operation of the aircraft at altitudes exceeding 6,000 m. At this stage of trials rapid increase and reduction of turbine RPM to minimum without the risk of compressor stall and engine flameout was impossible. The capability of increasing and reducing turbine RPM was often necessary in combat flying. The chief designer, V. I. Klimov, was obliged to design an automatic device, enabling flexible adjustment of engine operation regardless of speed and altitude. It was also ordered to install an autonomic engine startup system, independent from ground power sources. Although the number of shortcomings in the tested SD aircraft (MiG-15bis s/n 105015) was considerable, more advantages were seen. Therefore after the completion of the state trials it was decided that the "experimental frontline fighter with VK-1 engine, based on production MiG-15 aircraft has completed state evaluation with satisfactory results and may enter series production and service". However, deletion of all identified defects and implementation of improvements in the series production was required. On 1 June 1950 it was ordered to send the tested MiG-15 with VK-1 engine, after all modifications and improvements, for verification at GK NII VVS and then be treated as a production pattern in 1951.

In early June 1950 series production of MiG-15bis aircraft was launched in six factories: No.1 at Kuybyshev, No. 21 at Gorky, No. 31 at Tbilisi, No. 126 at Komsomolsk-on-Amur, No. 153 at Novosibirsk and No. 292 at Saratov. The aircraft's

[32+33]: MiG-15bis "376" (s/n 133076) during its service in Powidz-based 38. PLM. Posing for the photograph is 1st Lt Jerzy Kozarek. The shortened serial number 3076 is visible ahead of the tactical number. The landing light is placed in the air intake dividing wall, which was typical for MiG-15bis aircraft of production batches up to the 33rd inclusive.

design and equipment was still being improved. Implementing the orders of the government of 26 January and of the Ministry of Aircraft Industry of 24 January 1950 the OKB-155 embarked on studies on a night/all weather version of the aircraft. Two production MiG-15s built in No. 381 factory in Moscow were used. They received the factory designations *izdeliye* SA-1 and SA-2. The aircraft were equipped with an OSP-48 instrument landing system, ARK-5 "Amur" automatic direction finder (in lieu of RPKO-10M direction finder), radio signal receiver, RV-2 "Kristal" low-altitude radar altimeter, DGMK-3 gyromagnetic compass. The "Bariy-M" transponder was installed for cooperation with ground-based radars. The aircraft was fitted with the RSIU-3 VHF radio. The AFA-1M photo camera and the electric camera bay door actuator were deleted. In place of the camera bay the "Bari-M" and RV-2 "Kristal" systems were installed. Several modifications related to the installation of the VK-1 engine in lieu of the RD-45F and improvements recommended for series production were also made to the SA-1 aircraft (s/n 3810102). The factory trials, conducted during 4 February – 10 March 1950, showed that the OSR-48 instrument landing system worked properly, but the instrument panel had to be redesigned. Next the SA-1 was sent for state evaluation at GK NII VVS, conducted during 29–31 March. The results of the state evaluation were similar to those of the factory trials. The SA-2 was not sent for such evaluation. Soon at the OKB-155 two other aircraft, SA-3 and SA-4, were modified for further improvement of the OSP-48 instrument landing system. The trials were completed with success. In the summer of 1950 the RV-2 transmitter antenna was relocated from the fuselage to the lower wing surface, between the 17th and 20th rib. The receiver antenna was moved further forward, near No. 6 frame to protect it against damage by expended cartridge cases when the gun was fired. From early January 1951 on the receiver antenna was installed on the starboard wing between the 2nd and 3rd rib.

Still unsolved was aircraft's tendency to go into a descending turn, which required quick elimination. In the case of MiG-15bis, faster than the MiG-15 with similar wings and powered by less powerful RD-45F engine, the rolling moment increased along with the increase of speed. Simultaneously aileron forces on the stick increased. In case of the first production "bis" aircraft, overcoming these forces at the speeds of 960–980 km/h exceeded the pilot's ability to stop the roll and prevent the aircraft from going inverted. It made attaining maximum speed at altitudes below 3,000 m impossible. Due to these characteristics of the MiG-15bis aircraft, occurring near the maximum speed, in July 1950 No. 1 Factory at Kuybyshev failed to fulfill the production plan. The "bis" aircraft built were flown, but not delivered formally to the VVS (or paid for). This situation lasted until August and September, when the government's decision about limiting the maximum speed of the MiG-15bis was issued. By the order of the commanding officer of the VVS, from 11 September 1950 the maximum speed of MiG-15bis below 2,500 m was limited to 1,040 km/h until elimination of the aircraft's faulty flight characteristics.

Until the start of production of wings of increased stiffness, the tendency to go into a descending turn was avoided thanks to bending 40 mm wide adjustable metal bars, mounted on the trailing edges. It allowed countering aircraft's roll in flight by moving the control column by 1/3 of its movement range. Total explanation and overcoming the uncontrollable aircraft characteristics near maximum speed, concerning the aircraft from the S-3 prototype to production MiG-15bis, was not easy. It required a lot of time and research, but was necessary to avoid possible accidents and crashes. By the order of VVS command, from 9 August 1950 tests on three MiG-15 aircraft, serial numbers 53210345, 53210346 and 53210347 built by Gorky Factory No. 21, were conducted at GK NII VVS. Despite logging 66 hours and 20 minutes in 100 sorties in all three aircraft, the tendency to go into a descending turn was not explained, but the "Instruction of operation and flying technique of MiG-15 aircraft with RD-45F and VK-1 engines" was created. In fact it was methodology for preventing this phenomenon.

Research on the reasons for the uncontrolled handling of the aircraft with the loss of stability in flight at maximum speed was still conducted. A new wing design of increased stiffness and modifications to the wing attachment points were made. After introduction of the changes, increasing wing stiffness and installation of metal, 40 mm wide mechanically folding bars, called "knives", on the trailing edges at the flaps two MiG-15bis aircraft (s/nos 122040 and 122067), built in the Factory No. 1, were sent to GK NII VVS. The third aircraft sent for testing, (s/n 53210434) built by Factory No. 21, had only the "knives" installed. During testing in straight and level flight at altitudes exceeding 3,000–4,000 m the "*valezhka*" did not occur on any of the tested aircraft till they reached M=0.92. On two aircraft, s/n 122067 and s/n 53210434, the "*valezhka*" did not occur in straight and level flight at an altitude of 9,000–10,000 m until M=0.95. To totally eliminate uncontrolled roll of the MiG-15bis aircraft at speed limited to M=0.92, s/n 122058 with a new variant of stiffened wings was prepared. The increase of the wing stiffness was achieved by strengthening of the wing structure and increase of the wing and leading edge skin thickness. These changes made the wing heavier by 47 kg.

The MiG-15bis (s/n 1115341), built by Factory No. 153 in Novosibirsk, was fitted with autonomic engine startup system with 12-SAM-25 battery set installed in technical hatch. The ST-2-48 electric starter, used in the Il-28 bomber for VK-1 engine startup, was installed. This system allowed for ten engine startups and did not exclude startup with the use of a ground power cart (called "*telezhka*").

Apart from the advantages of these aircraft, extreme conditions of MiG-15 operation in Korea revealed, also several shortcomings. In early November 1950 the first MiG-15s of the 151. Fighter Aviation Division of the Guards appeared over North Korea. The first MiG-15bis aircraft of the 50th Fighter Aviation Division entered air combat on 30 November. December encounters with US fighters revealed a serious defect – weak construction of the rudder at the mass balance and vertical stabilizer attachment point. High speeds and g-loads in air combat often caused deformations of the rudder. In two instances deformation of the rudders and their possible destruction led to crashes and the loss of two pilots. With joint efforts of factory specialists and technical staff of the 50th Division these defects were removed on all the Division's "bis" aircraft. On the rudders and vertical stabilizers, at rudder attachment points and mass balances, reinforcing tabs were riveted. Rudders on 35 MiG-15bis aircraft were replaced. Admittedly there were some instances of rudder deformation in the 50th Division, but there were no crashes caused by weak empennage construction, neither in the 50th Division nor in the entire 64th Corps. Air combat revealed that the ASP-3N gunsights were inaccurate and did not guarantee accurate fire at speeds exceeding 800 km/h. In November 1952 improved ASR-3NM gunsights were installed. Mikoyan's design team reacted on remarks from Korea and introduced the necessary modifications to the design to eliminate the shortcomings revealed in combat. They were subsequently implemented in series production aircraft.

[34]: A pair of MiG-15bis fighters, "460" and "468" from Malbork-based 41. PLM.

[35]: MiG-15bis "464" (s/n 134064), with shortened serial number 4064. After the 41. PLM it was operated by the 31. PLM and then transferred to the 38. PLM based at Powidz. There it was operated until the regiment's disbandment in 1958. In 1959 it was on the strength of the 59. PSz-B based at Biała Podlaska.

To improve the fighter's accuracy air brakes of greater area (from 0.5 to 0.8 sq.m) were installed on MiG-15bis (s/n 53210668). The ejection process was facilitated to allow the pilot to eject using only the left or right hand in case of being wounded. It was also decided to retrofit the MiG-15bis aircraft of the 64th Independent Fighter Corps, operating in Korea, with improved ejection seats. Factories No. 1 and 153 were obliged to deliver 20 new seats and 312 sets of parts for modification of previously used seats. The deadline for completion of all Corps' aircraft by maintenance crews and factory teams in repair units was set for 13 August 1952. Apart from the commencement of series production of the "bis" aircraft with enlarged airbrakes, it was also ordered to retrofit the aircraft of the 64th Corps with the new airbrakes with the aid of No. 1 and No. 153 factory teams by 19 September. Moreover, Factory No. 153 was obliged to retrofit 60 aircraft with new RSIU-3 VHF wireless sets, compatible with RAS-UKW ground-based radios.

MiG-15bis aircraft were produced until 1953 by factories in Kuybyshev, Gorky, Tbilisi, Komsomolsk-on-Amur, Novosibirsk and Saratov. Production totaled 7,936 examples.

Factory No. 21 in Gorky launched production of MiG-15bisR (type 55) reconnaissance aircraft simultaneously with the MiG-15bis. From s/n 55210101 the MiG-15bisR aircraft were equipped with an AFA-BA/40 vertical photo camera. It underwent testing and was recommended for tactical reconnaissance. It was capable of photographing a strip of terrain 0.9–4.5 km wide from an altitude of 2,000 to 10,000 m at a distance of 90 to 450 km. Production MiG-15bisR aircraft were armed with one N-37 and one NR-23 cannon and powered by the VK-1 engine. During 1951–1952 a total of 364 MiG-15bisR tactical reconnaissance aircraft were built.

By the end of 1951 Factory No. 292 in Saratov built 49 MiG-15bisS escort fighters. These longer range aircraft were intended for escort of bomber and troop transport aircraft. Numerous prototypes and experimental aircraft were built in order enhance the fighter's combat capability, improve equipment and strengthen the armament. Five MiG-15Pbis aircraft with Toriy-A radar, intended for pilot training, were built.

In Poland

In December 1952 MiG-15bis fighters purchased in the USSR arrived in Poland. The aircraft were delivered in crates by rail to Malbork. After assembly the aircraft were flown by Soviet pilots. They were assigned to three regiments – 1. PLM of the 5. DLM, 28. PLM of the 10. DLM and 41. PLM of the 9. DLM. The MiG-15bis aircraft entered the inventory of these units on 22 and 23 January 1953.

The 1. PLM received four MiG-15bis aircraft, serial numbers: 133011, 133027, 133068 and 133096.

The 28. PLM received 11 aircraft, serial numbers: 125054, 133030, 133046, 133051, 133059, 133063, 133073, 133076, 133088, 133095, 133098. (s/n 133095 was assigned to the staff flight of the 10. DLM).

The 41. PLM received 15 aircraft, serial numbers: 133052, 134015, 134060, 134064, 134066(?), 134068, 134069, 136015, 136035, 136045, 136047, 136060, 136061, 136067 and 136069.

The latest (and secret) MiG-15bis fighters were assigned to the units that were were intended to serve on the northern

[36+37]: MiG-15bis "464" (s/n 134064), ended its service with the Air Force Technical School (TSWL) at Zamość. To the shortened serial number 4064, visible on the landing gear door, the symbol "1B0", as on a Lim-2, was quite crudely added. So the fake serial number 1B 04 064 was created, which may suggest that 64 Lim-2 aircraft of the 4th production batch were built. This aircraft was handed over from Zamość to a memorial in Starachowice.

[38]: MiG-15bis "554" (s/n 125054). It entered service in the 28. PLM, from which it was transferred to the 1. PLM and replaced with an older MiG-15. Next it was transferred to the 61. PLM-Sz based at Piła. It ended its service in the 58. LPSz-B based at Dęblin.

38

[39]: MiG-15bis "615" (s/n 136015). During 1956–1958 it was operated by Powidz-based 38. PLM. 1st Lt Henryk Sygnowski is posing in the cockpit. In 1959 the aircraft was on the strength of the 59. PSz-B based at Biała Podlaska.

frontiers of the country. The level of secrecy protecting the "bis" fighters is shown by special, increased level of security of the 1st Squadron of Malbork-based 41. PLM. The MiG-15bis fighters stood on a separate sector of the flightline, surrounded by barbed wire and guarded by armed sentries.

The purchased "bis" fighters had the last four digits of the serial number painted on the fuselage. This four-digit number omitted the first digit "1", denoting Kuybyshev-based Factory No.1, and the first digit of the number of the production batch. Among thirty Polish MiG-15bis aircraft there were also examples with two-digit tactical numbers, such as "96", on which the last two digits of the serial number 3096 are painted on the forward fuselage. Most "bis" aircraft flew with three-digit tactical numbers, related to the serial numbers. For instance, the MiG-15bis with the serial number 3052 painted received the tactical number "352". Later on Polish "bis" aircraft four-digit tactical numbers, identical with the last four digits of the serial number, could be seen, as on "3068" operated at Krzesiny air base. The newest of thirty MiG-15bis aircraft, delivered in December 1952, was the 68th example of the 37th production batch, built that year. It was marked with the shortened number (7068) and its full serial number was 137068. The oldest of the delivered "bis" aircraft had the serial number 125054. It was built in February 1951 and came from the 25th production batch. Aircraft from the 33rd, 34th and 36th production batches were newer. They were built in February and March 1952. The largest number of delivered MiG-15bis aircraft came from the 33rd batch. Four of them entered service in the 1. PLM, nine were assigned to the 28. PLM and only one "bis" of the 33rd batch was delivered to the 41. PLM. It was MiG-15bis tactical number "352" (s/n 133052).

In some sources information can be found that the MiG-15 fighters had the landing light mounted in the dividing wall of the air intake, which differed from the MiG-15bis, which had this light mounted under the port wing. It is not entirely true. Individual batches of MiG-15 and MiG-15bis aircraft differed between each other in details. MiG-15bis aircraft up to the 33rd batch inclusive had the landing light mounted in the air intake dividing wall, like the MiG-15. Among Polish "bis" aircraft there was one of the 25th batch and 14 of the 33rd batch, which had the landing light in the upper part of the dividing wall, such as for instance (s/n 133052), tactical number "352" and (s/n 133076), tactical number "376". From the 34th batch on the landing light was relocated to the port wing. Polish "bis" aircraft with tactical numbers "468" and "635" had landing lights on the port wing.

On 5 March 1953 1st Lt Franciszek Jarecki of Słupsk-based 28. PLM made a bold escape to Bornholm in MiG-15bis "346" (s/n 133046). Adding sensational piquancy to this event was the fact that this 21-year old pilot did this risky feat in one of eleven new MiG-15bis fighters, which had entered the regiment's inventory a mere few weeks earlier. Moreover, the date of the escape became symbolic because on that day Joseph Stalin died.

1st Lt Jarecki took off at 0655 hours on a patrol mission in a two-ship formation with 1st Lt Józef Caputa. Making use of heavy overcast on that day he separated from 1st Lt Caputa and jettisoned his underwing fuel tanks, which decreased the aircraft's drag and weight. He descended to 200 m in a steep dive to avoid being detected by radar. Initial suspicions of Jarecki's superiors that he had died gave way to suspicion of escape, when Soviet MiGs sent to search the sea found the jettisoned fuel tanks. The MiG-15bis "346" landed safely at the small airfield near Rønne, the capital of Bornholm. It was inspected by Western specialists and returned to Poland.

On 9 April 1953, during night flights in the 28. PLM, 1st Lt Czajka lost orientation, could not return to Redzikowo air base and ejected from an airworthy aircraft. The first advanced MiG-15bis fighter, "388" (s/n 133088), was lost.

Fifteen days later, on 24 April, this time in the 41. PLM, another MiG-15bis "469" (s/n 134069) was damaged. It stalled about 8 meters above the runway. After this accident the aircraft was sent to the Repair Depot at Bemowo airfield.

Soon another escape by a Polish pilot to Bornholm took place. This happened on 25 May 1953 in Malbork-based 41. PLM. At 0710 hours two MiG-15bis aircraft of the Quick Reaction Alert flight took off. 1st Lt Roman Lachcik was the flight leader and 2nd Lt Zdzisław Jaźwiński flew wing. The QRA flight was scrambled because of a bogey, which flew into Polish airspace. It was a Soviet bomber aircraft, which was simulating violation of the border. 2nd Lt Jaźwiński did not join the flight leader, but descended, heading to Bornholm. He made an emergency wheels-up landing. The MiG-15bis "415" (s/n 134015) of 2nd Lt Jaźwiński was severely damaged. After hitting a pile of stones and small trees the starboard wing and tailplane were damaged, but the pilot was not hurt. After another successful escape of a Polish pilot severe repression affected his family and the personnel of the Malbork-based regiment. Three squadron commanders in the 41. PLM were arrested and sentenced to 12 years in prison (they were released in 1956). The regiment commander was replaced and many pilots were sent to other garrisons. Another result of the escapes was intensified development of secret services in the military and recruitment of secret informers. Aircraft exchange was made – the MiG-15bis aircraft were redeployed from Malbork and Słupsk inland, to three regiments of the 5. DLM: 1. PLM, 13. PLM and 31. PLM. In the staff flights of 9. and 10. DLM headquarters only individual MiG-15bis aircraft were left. These fighters, a bit faster that the MiG-15s, could be useful in chasing other potential fugitives from Pomerania. In the regiments based near the coast underwing tanks were not installed and the aircraft were not refuelled to "full".

In return for the MiG-15bis three regiments of Warsaw-based 5. DLM transferred older, weary and slower MiG-15 aircraft to Słupsk- and Malbork-based regiments. For instance, during the exchange of the "bis" with MiG-15s the 1. PLM accepted and took on strength on 26 May the MiG-15bis aircraft with following tactical: "554" (s/n 125054), "330" (s/n 133030), "395" (s/n 133095) and "398" (s/n 133098). The following MiG-15s were ferried to the 28. PLM: in May s/nos 0234 and 0237 and in June s/nos 1238, 1328 and 1340. From the Malbork-based regiment the following three MiG-15bis aircraft were ferried and taken on strength of the 1. PLM on 27 May: "615" (s/n 136015), "647" (s/n 136047) and "669"

[40]: MiG-15bis "615". Initially it probably had the two-digit tactical number "61", as the wider shape of the digit "5" indicates.

[41]: MiG-15bis "635" (s/n 136035), of the 62. PSz-T LM, Poznań-Krzesiny air base, 1956. Posing on the ladder is the regiment's CO, Capt. Andrzej Dobrzeniecki.

[42]: MiG-15bis "645" (s/n 136045). It initially was operated by the 41. PLM, then 31. PLM (Warsaw-Bemowo). In 1956 it was transferred to the 38. PLM, where it was operated until the regiment's disbandment in 1958. It was flown several times by 2nd Lt Bolesław Jeska.

(s/n 136069). Three MiG-15s, 0306, 1316 and 1338, were ferried to the Malbork-based 41. PLM.

In June 1953 redeployment of the 13. PLM from Bemowo airfield, previously occupied by three regiments, to the airfield at Leźnica Wielka near Łęczyca began. The 1. PLM, still based at Bemowo, after completion of autumn preparation work for winter operations had 15 fighter aircraft, including 12 MiG-15bis and three MiG-15s. Shortages of aircraft were expected to be made up with domestic production. The third regiment of the 5. DLM, the 31. PLM had 12 MiG-15bis and two MiG-15 aircraft in its inventory on 1 October 1953.

In 1956 the 38. PLM was formed at Powidz air base. The airfield, previously a base of the Soviet strategic bomber force, was left by a regiment of Tu-16 bombers. The new Polish fighter regiment was formed on the basis of a squadron from Mierzęcice-based 39. PLM, equipped with Lim-2 aircraft, redeployed from Mierzęcice on 13 September 1956. The mainstay of the new regiment were Lim-2 aircraft. The regiment's strength was complemented with MiG-15bis fighters, previously operated by the 1. PLM and 31. PLM. In mid-December 1956 on the strength of the Powidz-based regiment were 17 Lim-2 and 8 MiG-15bis aircraft. During an air show on 8 September 1957, in which 300 aircraft were engaged, fighters of the 38. PLM also took part. Twenty-five aircraft from Powidz made a flypast in parade formation. In the column of five five-ship flights of Lim-2 and MiG-15bis aircraft in "herringbone" formation were six MiG-15bis aircraft. During two years of the of regiment's existence it received the following MiG-15bis aircraft: "376" (s/n 133076), "410" (s/n 134010), "460" (s/n 134060), "464" (s/n 134064), "615" (s/n 136015), "635" (s/n 136035), "645" (s/n 136045), "647" (s/n 136047), "660" (s/n 136060), "61" (s/n 136061), "647" (s/n 136047) and "669" (s/n 136069). After two years the Powidz-based 38. PLM was disbanded and some of the personnel and aircraft were assigned to then-forming Advanced Flying School at Modlin.

The MiG-15bis were withdrawn from combat to training units. On 25 June 1960 there was a crash of a MiG-15bis from the 61. PSz-B (*Pułk Szkolno Bojowy* – Combat Training Regiment) at Nowe Miasto nad Pilicą. Second Lieutenant Henryk Brzuszkiewicz was flying a night interception sortie in good weather. Due to pilot error when making a turn the aircraft crashed in woods near the village of Prosna. The fuel tanks exploded and the pilot was killed.

The last crash of a MiG-15bis took place in the Dęblin-based 58. PSz-B on 27 March 1961. When 1st Lt Stanisław Kocik was returning from a night cross-country sortie in bad weather, the cloud base was 300 m and a snowfall occurred. The pilot was not qualified to fly in bad weather, yet he was not sent to an alternate airfield. The MiG-15bis "647" (s/n 136047) crashed in woods near the village of Piskory. The pilot was killed.

As the deliveries of the new Lim-2 aircraft to Air Defence fighter regiments progressed, they were assigned to the 1st Squadrons, while the 2nd Squadrons still operated older Lim-1s. The 3rd Squadrons, which had the training role, operated MiG-15bis and S-102 aircraft. The MiG-15bis aircraft withdrawn from fighter or attack regiments ended their service in the training regiments. On 1 December 1959 the 59. PSz-B at Biała Podlaska, among 74 aircraft in its inventory, had two MiG-15bis aircraft: "464" (s/n 134064) and "615" (s/n 136015) and one MiG-15, "39" (s/n 119074).

MiG-15bis fighters delivered to Poland, serial numbers: 125054, 133011, 133027, 133030, 133046, 133051, 133052, 133059**,

133063, 133068, 133073, 133076, 133088, 133095, 133096, 133098, 134015, 134060, 134064, 134066, 134068, 134069, 136015, 136035, 136045, 136047, 136060, 136061, 136067, 136069, 137086*.

** One more, the 31st MiG-15bis, s/n 137086 was delivered to Poland. It came from the last, 37th batch from the Kuybyshev plant. It was sent to the WSK Mielec factory as the pattern for Lim-2 aircraft production. Next it was transferred to the Institute of Aviation, where it was used for various research flights with the registration SP-GLZ. It was used for flying tests of reusable parachute containers for supersonic aerial targets. It was written off the civil aviation register on 4 November 1972.*

*** The MiG-15bis s/n 133059 was converted to a two-seat SBLim-2 trainer in No.2 Military Aircraft Repair Works in 1974. Th forward fuselage section from SBLim-1 s/n 1A-12002 was used for the conversion.*

Two MiG-15bis aircraft were lost in crashes, one was destroyed due to a failure. There is no information, whether "469"/134069 from the 41. PLM, which after having stalled 8 meters above ground and was sent to the repair depot at Bemowo airfield, returned to service.

[43]: MiG-15bis "3068" in the 51. PLM-Sz based at Piła, with altered shape of the tactical number digits.

44]: MiG-15bis "352" (s/n 3052) from the 41. PLM based at Malbork airfield, probably 1953s

[45]: MiG-15bis "96" (s/n 3096). In January 1953 it entered service in the 1. PLM.

[46]: MiG-15bis "96" (s/n 3096). The aircraft is in natural metal finish with transparent lacquer coating. In the 1. PLM it wore a two-digit tactical number with wide digits and the gaps after removal of the stencil not painted over. The serial number was black.

47 *[47]: MiG-15bis "352" (s/n 3052). The aircraft is in natural metal finish with transparent lacquer coating. Like most MiG-15bis aircraft in this regiment it wore a three-digit tactical number. PTB-260 underwing tanks had the capacity of 260 litres each.*

a.m.olejniczak '21

48

49

[48+49]: MiG-15bis "352", with shortened serial number 3052 visible. (The complete serial number was 133052). It was delivered to Malbork-based 41. PLM on 23 January 1953.

50

[50]: MiG-15bis “3068” (s/n 3068) of the 62. PSz-T LM, Poznań-Krzesiny air base. The aircraft is in natural metal finish with transparent lacquer coating, except for the air brakes and steel gun blast shields, and carries 300-litre PTB 300 underwing tanks. The tactical number was red, identical with the last four digits of the serial number. Note the shape of the digit “8”.

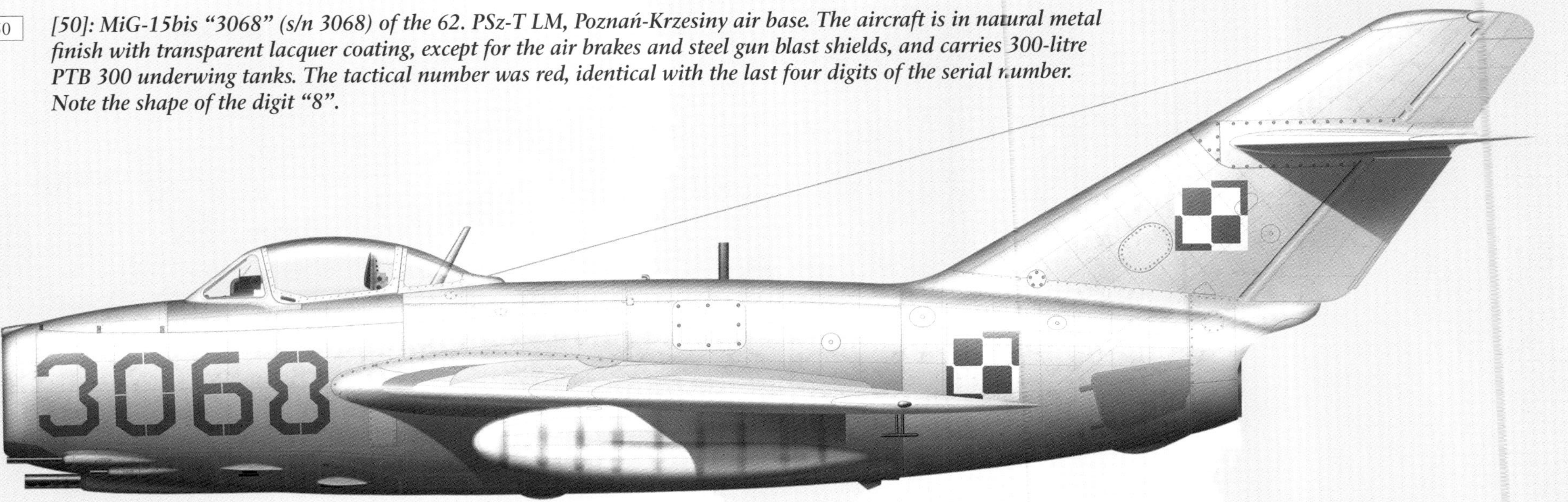

51

[51]: MiG-15bis “3068” (s/n 3068), of the 62. PSz-T LM, Poznań-Krzesiny air base, 1956. The tactical number was identical with the last four digits of the serial number.

52

[52]: MiG-15bis (s/n 137086), operated by the Institute of Aviation in Warsaw. The tail was painted yellow in the Institute. It wore the civil registration SP-GLZ until being struck off the register on 4 November 1972.

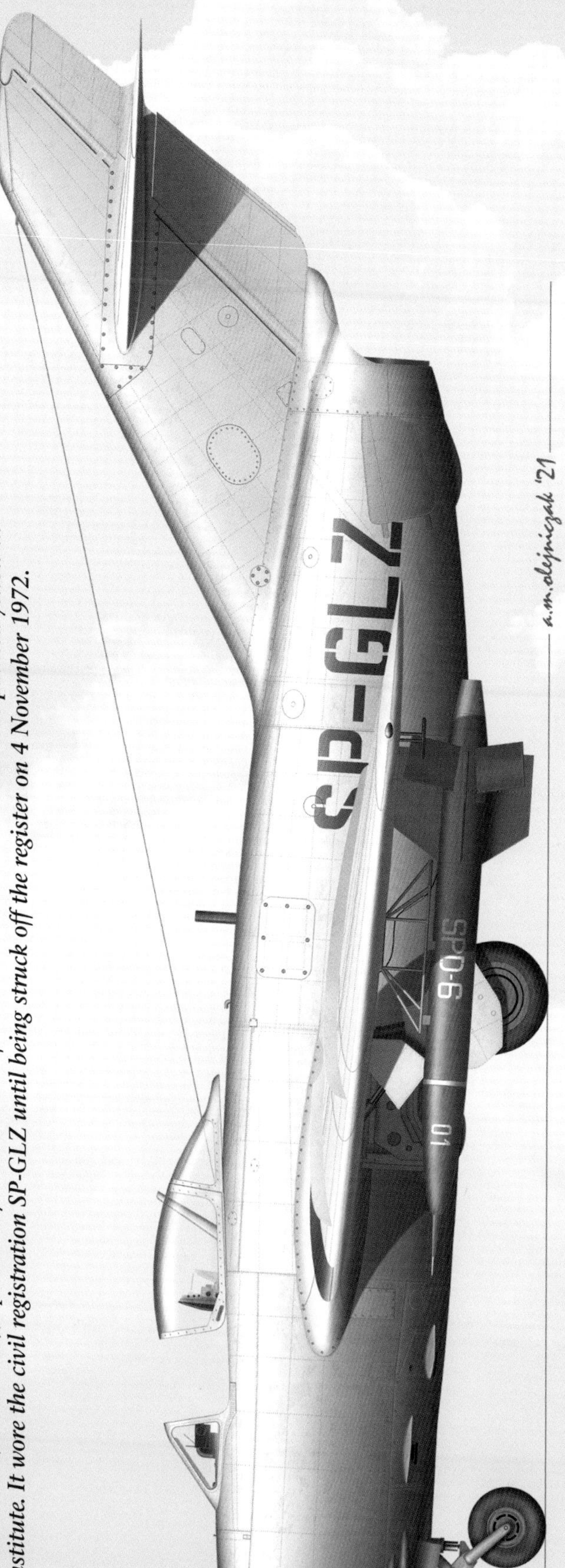
SP-GLZ
SPD-6
01
a.m.olejniczak '21

53

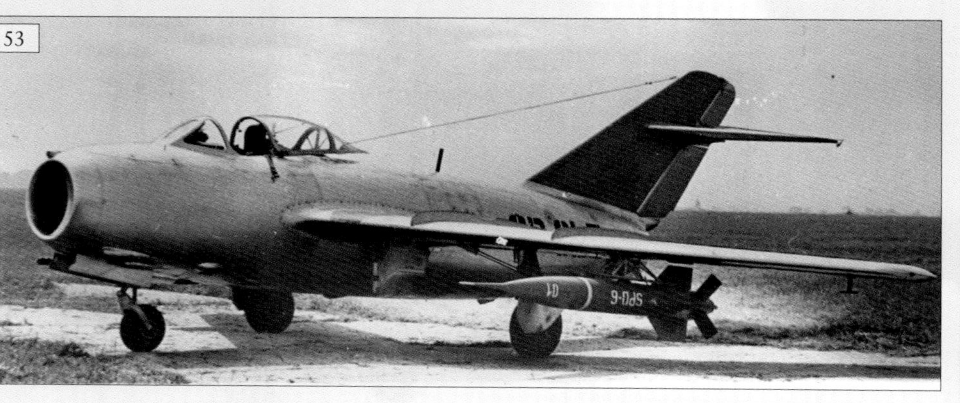

SPD-6
01

54

SP-GLZ

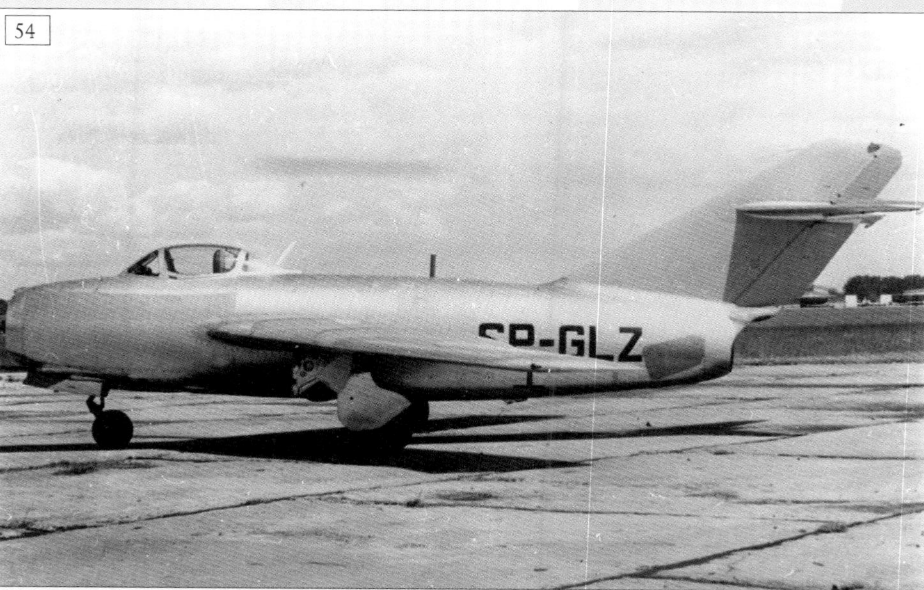

[53+54]: MiG-15bis (s/n 137086) was delivered to the WSK Mielec factory as a pattern aircraft. After being transferred to the Institute of Aviation in 1958 it received the civil registration SP-GLZ and the tailfin was painted yellow. Under the wing an SPD-6 pod is mounted.

S-102

S-102 was the designation given to the MiG-15 in Czechoslovakia (S comes from the Czech word "*stihac*", which means fighter). When the Soviet factories were ending their two-year long production of the MiG-15 in 1950 and switching to production of the upgraded MiG-15bis, the Soviet authorities allowed for production of these aircraft in Czechoslovakia and then in Poland. In 1952 the USSR delivered 62 of these aircraft from Soviet fighter regiments based in East Germany to Czechoslovakia. The contract for license production of the MiG-15 was signed in Moscow on 17 April 1951. In the next month transfer of the production documentation started and on 6 May the latest aircraft (s/n 119070) from the Kuybyshev factory, was delivered. It was the pattern for MiG-15 assembly. Soon the Letov factory at Letnany received 10 sets of aircraft components for assembly. The first of the pre-production aircraft, assembled from Soviet parts (s/n 225101), was flown on

[55]: S-102 "60" (s/n 231660) of the 40. PLM based at Świdwin. Initially the S-102 received two-digit tactical numbers, which were the last two digits of the serial number.

[56]: A commemorative photograph of the S-102 "68 " from Wrocław-based 3. PLM. The serial number 231865 is visible on the gun fairings.

57

[57]: S-102 "72" (s/n 231872) operated by Wrocław-based 3. PLM.

58

59 [58+59]: S-102 "73" (s/n 231873), operated by the 1st Squadron of No. 4 Officer Flying Training School. 1st Lt Bogdan Rudygier trained on it. Nowe Miasto and Pilicą air base, 1957.

6 November 1951. After having built 160 S-102 fighters in the Letnany-based factory, in July 1953 the production was relocated to the Aero factory at Vodochody. In total, both factories built 821 S-102 aircraft in 12 production batches.

In 1953 delays in the Lim-1 aircraft deliveries led to a difficult situation in Polish fighter units. The 40. PLM, part of the 7. DLM, based at Mierzęcice, which operated 13 Yak-23 aircraft and only one UTIMiG-15 combat trainer, was moved to Świdwin on 23 January 1953. It was planned to re-equip it with the Lim-1. Long delays in deliveries of the Lim-1 fighters from the WSK Mielec factory led to an emergency purchase of the MiG-15 fighters licence-built in Czechoslovakia as the S-102. While the Mielec factory was initially producing a few aircraft per month, in Poland's southern neighbour the production of the S-102 aircraft was in full swing. To make up for fighter aircraft shortages, sixty S-102 fighters were purchased in Czechoslovakia in two transactions. Wrocław-based 3. PLM received 16 aircraft of this batch and 14 were delivered to the Świdwin-based 40. PLM. The last aircraft of this batch was assigned to the staff flight of the 11. DLM at Świdwin, then being formed. In late November 1953 another batch of 12 S-102 aircraft was delivered to Poland and assigned to the 26. PLM, based at Zegrze Pomorskie. In late 1953 and early 1954 the last 17 S-102 fighters were delivered to Poland. They were divided

[60]: S-102 "87" operated by Wrocław-based 3. PLM. The serial number 231887 is visible on the N-37 cannon fairing.

[61]: S-102 "77" (s/n 231877) operated by Wrocław-based 3. PLM.

[62]: *S-102 of the 61. LPSz-B with stylized number "91". Nowe Miasto and Pilicą air base, 1958.*

[63]: *S-102 "501" (s/n 231501) entered service in the 26. PLM based at Zegrze Pomorskie. The tactical number consists of the last three digits of the serial number.*

64

[64]: S-102 "504" (s/n 231504) operated by Malbork-based 41. PLM.

65

[65+66]: S-102 "669" (s/n 231669) at Radom-Sadków air base in 1958.

66

between the 3. PLM, 40. PLM and 26. PLM, except for one aircraft assigned to the staff flight of the headquarters of the 3. MKL (*Mieszany Korpus Lotniczy* – Composite Air Corps), based in Poznań, former 3. KLM (*Korpus Lotnictwa Mysliwskiego* – Fighter Aviation Corps), renamed in 1956).

The S-102 fighters delivered to Poland received initially two-digit red tactical numbers, related to the ending of the serial number, for instance the S-102 (s/n 231860) from the 40. PLM, which had the tactical number "60". Another aircraft from this regiment (s/n 231891), received the tactical number "91". Later the S-102 aircraft received three-digit tactical numbers. These were the last three digits of the serial numbers. For instance, S-102 (s/n 231862) had the tactical number "862".

The beginning of S-102 service in the Polish units was troubled. Technical problems occurred, resulting in crashes and failures. The first crash took place on 28 August 1955 during night flights in bad weather in Wrocław-based 3. PLM. 2nd Lt Bolesław Orłowski was flying in a two-ship formation in S-102 "890" (s/n 231890). After 8–9 minutes of flight the aircraft went into a dive and crashed near the village of Dobroszyce. The pilot probably lost consciousness due to wrong pressurization of the cockpit.

The S-102 fighters delivered to the 40. PLM initially caused technical problems due to the short time between overhauls of engines and frequent failures of the hydraulic systems. In 1956 there were two crashes of the S-102 aircraft in Świdwin-based

[67]: S-102 "674" (s/n 231674) of the 41. PLM, with 1st Lt Pawulski posing on the ladder. This aircraft was previously operated by the 26. PLM, based at Zegrze Pomorskie.

[68]: S-102 "673" (s/n 231673).

40. PLM, in which two pilots were killed. The first crash occurred on 13 March. 1st Lt Stanisław Chalimoniuk lost spatial orientation after having flown into the clouds during a cross country flight. The S-102 „846" (s/n 231846) crashed in an inverted position near the village of Kłopotowo, in the district of Kołobrzeg.

The second crash took place on 18 December 1956, during an aerial gunnery training sortie. 2nd Lt Marian Pałka took off in S-102 "860" (s/n 231860) as the wingman of 1st Lt Choiński. Having attained an altitude of 2,500 m he began to execute the task. After the third firing pass the aircraft probably went into spin, crashed near the village of Drozdowo and burned. The pilot was killed.

In the mid-1960s a considerable number of S-102 aircraft was transferred from fighter regiments to attack units, converting to jet aircraft. Several S-102 aircraft ended their service in training regiments. In the 61. PSz-B, based at Nowe Miasto and Pilicą, bad luck persecuted the S-102 "66" (s/n 231866). First, in April 1961 it was damaged due to pilot error on landing. The aircraft was repaired and returned to service. Two months later, on 20 June 1961 when the aircraft was flown by 2nd Lt Lucjan Ziemkowski, the engine cut out twice. The pilot landed with a dead engine at Tomaszów Mazowiecki airfield. "66" was destroyed after touchdown on the far end of the runway, hitting the embankment. The pilot was taken to hospital.

In Radom-based 60. Psz-B, S-102 "882" (s/n 231882) collided with the target drogue during an aerial gunnery sortie on 14 June 1961, damaging the nose section. The aircraft was repaired and returned to service.

It was not possible to return to service the S-102 "660"/231660 from the 58. PSz-B. During taxiing before take-off on 28 July 1965 at Dęblin air base an explosion and fire in the aft fuselage section occurred. The pilot managed to stop the engine and abandon the aircraft. The fire was extinguished, but the rear fuselage with engine were burned out. The fire was caused by improper maintenance of the fuel system during a routine check. The aircraft was scrapped.

S-102 fighters delivered to Poland, serial numbers: 231602, 231842, 231846, 231847, 231848, 231850, 231851, 231852, 231853, 231854, 231855, 231856, 231857, 231858, 231859, 231860, 231861, 231862, 231863, 231864, 231865, 231866, 231867*, 231868, 231869, 231870, 231871, 231872, 231873, 231875, 231877, 231881, 231882, 231884, 231887, 231889, 231890, 231891, 231892, 231897, 231501, 231504, 231627, 231639, 231651, 231655, 231656, 231658, 231660, 231661, 231663, 231669, 231671, 231672, 231673, 231674, 231677, 231682, 231695, 231697.

** The S-102 (s/n 231867) was converted to SBLim-2 combat trainer at No. 2 Military Aircraft Repair Works during November 1973-April 1974. After the conversion it retained the serial number of the S-102 fighter.*

Three S-102 aircraft were lost in crashes and two were scrapped following failures.

[69]: S-102 "859" (s/n 231859) at the base of the 61. LPSz-B in Nowe Miasto. It entered service on 18 September 1953 in the 3. PLM OPL based at Wrocław. Later it was operated by training regiments. First it was operated by Radom-based 60. LPSz-B. It was retired from the Nowe Miasto-based regiment in May 1964.

69

70

[70]: S-102 "869" (s/n 231869).

[71]: S-102 "862" (s/n 231862). The serial number is painted on the forward fuselage, vertical stabilizer and rudder.

71

72

[72]: S-102 "91" (s/n 231891) from the 2nd Combat Training Squadron of Radom-based OSL-5, Radom-Sadków air base, spring of 1957. The aircraft is in natural metal finish with transparent lacquer coating. Two-digit tactical number was identical with the last two digits of the serial number.

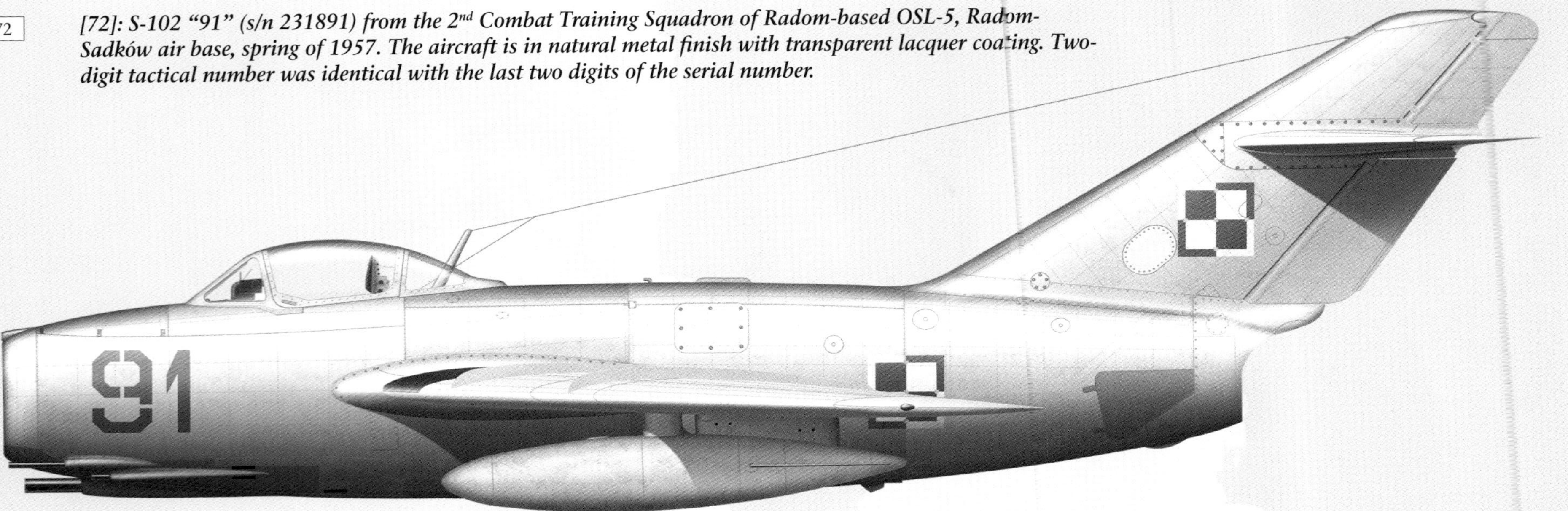

73

[73]: S-102 "91" (s/n 231891), Radom-Sadków air base, spring of 1957.

74

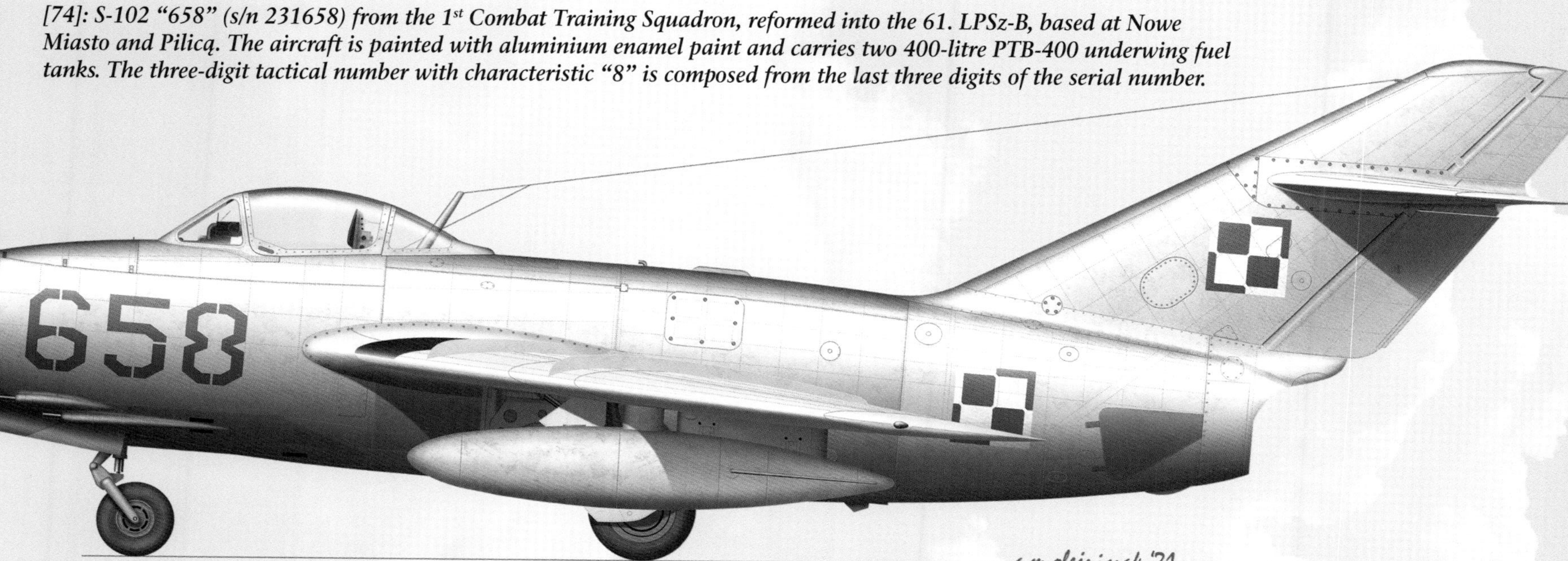

[74]: S-102 "658" (s/n 231658) from the 1st Combat Training Squadron, reformed into the 61. LPSz-B, based at Nowe Miasto and Pilicą. The aircraft is painted with aluminium enamel paint and carries two 400-litre PTB-400 underwing fuel tanks. The three-digit tactical number with characteristic "8" is composed from the last three digits of the serial number.

75

[75]: S-102 "658" (s/n 231658), operated by the 61. LPSz-B, based at Nowe Miasto nad Pilicą.

Lim-1 (1A)

The MiG-15 aircraft built in Poland under Soviet license were designated Lim-1 (*licencyjny myśliwiec pierwszy*, which means Licence Fighter One). They were also referred to as "product C", after Russian nomenclature. In the USSR the MiG-15 aircraft were referred to as "product S" (in the Russian alphabet it is C). The Lim-1 was the first jet-powered aircraft built in Poland. It received the factory designation 1A. At the end of 1949/early1950 licence production of the Yak-17 fighter, designated G-1 in Poland, was being considered. The Yak-17 was powered by an RD-10 engine (clone of the German Junkers Jumo 004, rated at 8,83 kN of thrust and time between overhauls of 25 hours). The idea of Yak-17 production was abandoned, because in early 1950 the possibility of production of the more capable Yak-23 fighter with RD-500 engine (an unlicensed copy of British Rolls-Royce Derwent V) in Poland appeared. The genuine British engine was rated at 15.6 kN of thrust and had a TBO of 180 hours. The RD-500 had a TBO of 100 hours. Preparatory work for licence production of the Yak-23 under the designation G-2 at WSK Mielec began. The work was at an advanced stage, but in the spring of 1951 was halted. In the USSR, when MiG-15 fighter production was being terminated in favour of the more advanced MiG-15bis, a decision was made about granting a licence for the production of the MiG-15 fighter, powered by RD-45F engine (unlicensed Soviet copy of British Rolls-Royce Nene II engine, rated at 22.26 kN of thrust). This decision was caused by the deteriorating world political and military situation after the outbreak of the Korean War. In May 1951 transfer of technical documentation of the aircraft, initially designated G-3, to the WSK Mielec factory began. Licence production was contracted to two factories: WSK (*Wytwórnia Sprzętu Komunikacyjnego* – Transportation Equipment Factory) WSK No. 1 at Mielec and WSK No. 5 at Świdnik. Final assembly was to be done in Mielec, and production of the wings, empennage, engine mount, gun tray and ejection seat was placed in Świdnik. WSK Rzeszów was tasked with RD-45F engine production under the designation Lis-1 (*Licencyjny silnik pierwszy* – licence engine one). Production of aircraft components was sub-contracted to cooperating factories. WSK Hydral of Wrocław manufactured the hydraulic system components and WSK Krosno produced the landing gear. WSK

[76]: Lim-1 "01" (s/n 1A01003) (third aircraft of the first production batch). It entered service in the 31. PLM based at Warsaw Bemowo/Babice airfield in September 1952.

[77]: Lim-1 "01" (s/n 1A11001) (first aircraft of the 11th production batch), operated by Świdwin-based 19. LEH during 1954–1958. It also sports the tactical number "01", although it is a different aircraft.

[78]: Lim-1s "97", "04" and "89" of the 5. DLM at Warsaw Bemowo/Babice airfield.

Warszawa II, existing from 1952, supplied components of the electric system and flight instruments. The design of the Lim-1 included numerous advanced technical solutions and new technologies were applied. New high-durability steel types were used for production of load-bearing components, such as fittings, wing spars and landing gear struts.

In early May 1952 assembly of five aircraft from parts delivered from the USSR began. They comprised the first pre-production batch, with serial numbers 1A-01001 through 1A-01005. On 26 September 1952 the initial four Lim-1 aircraft were delivered to Bemowo airfield. They were assigned to four units of the 5. DLM. Aircraft (s/n 1A-01001) was assigned to the 13. PLM, (s/n 1A-01002) was assigned to the 1. PLM on the same day, and the third one (s/n 1A-01003), was assigned to the 31. PLM, where it received the tactical number "01". Five Lim-1 aircraft from the initial batch, assembled from Soviet parts, received red tactical numbers "01" through "05". These numbers were not fragments of the serial numbers. The last of the four Lim-1s delivered (s/n 1A-01004), was assigned to the staff flight of the 5. DLM headquarters. The fifth aircraft of the first production batch (s/n 1A-01005), was flown as late as March 1953. By the end of December 1952 only two aircraft of the second batch had been assembled: (s/n 1A-02001) and (s/n 1A-02002). They were flown in January 1953. They were ferried to the 31. PLM based at Warsaw Bemowo-Babice airfield on 30 January 1953. On 27 February a further two Lim-1 aircraft, (s/n 1A-02003) and (s/n 1A-03001), were also assigned to the 31. PLM. For March delivery of five aircraft was planned, but only four had been completed: (1A-02004), (1A-03002), (1A-03003) and (1A-03004). Aircraft (s/n 1A-01005) was declared as the fifth example, lacking in the monthly plan, and it was recorded in the fulfilled March monthly production plan as "production pattern".

The first two Lim-1 aircraft assigned to the 34. PLM MW (*Pułk Lotnictwa Myśliwskiego Marynarki Wojennej* – Naval Fighter Aviation Regiment) landed at Babie Doły air base on 1 April 1953. Lt Romuald Rozmysłowicz and LtJG Marian Piątek ferried two Lim-1 fighters from Bemowo/Babice airfield: "8" (s/n 1A-02003) and "12" (s/n 1A-02004). The stand of the new aircraft was fenced off with barbed wire and for a week access to them was granted only to the commanding staff of the 33. DLM MW (*Dywizja Lotnictwa Myśliwskiego Marynarki Wojennej* – Naval Aviation Division), pilots and selected maintenance crews. During the next few days further Lim-1 aircraft of the 3rd production batch arrived.

On 5 September 1953 five Lim-1 aircraft of the August production run were delivered to the 25. PLM, based at Pruszcz Gdański. Four aircraft (s/nos 1A-05006 through 1A-05009) were from the 5th production batch. Aircrat (s/n 1A-06001) was the first example of the 6th batch. In September 1953 the planned production tempo of Lim-1 aircraft was increased and 15 aircraft of the 6th batch were built. One aircraft of this batch (s/n 1A-06016) was assigned to the 5. DLM. As result, in late September 1953 fifteen aircraft were delivered to the 25. PLM. They joined five aircraft of the August production run, delivered previously. Thanks to these deliveries the 25. PLM became the first regiment of the Polish air arm equipped solely with aircraft of Polish production. They were powered by RD-45F engines of Soviet manufacture. Only the next lot of nine aircraft from the sixth production batch (s/nos 1A-06018 – 1A-06026) was of entirely Polish production, with licence-built Lis-1 engines from WSK Rzeszów. (The first of them (s/n 1A-06018), was selected on 26 October for state evaluation and type approval. After having reached the maximum ceiling, when the aircraft flown by Maj. Ostrowski was approaching landing, the engine quit. The pilot managed to make an emergency landing, touching down short of the end of the runway. The Lim-1 (s/n 1A-06018) with broken landing gear stopped on the barbed wire fence. The pilot survived. The failure was caused by accidental fuel cut-off when the pilot was pulling the landing gear lever. The necessary minor design changes were introduced in the cockpits in MiG-15 and Lim-1 aircraft to prevent such accidents in the future. In 1954 in the inventory of the 25. PLM had 18 Lim-1 aircraft. Among them were five examples of the 5th batch, (s/nos 1A-05006 – 1A-05010) with tactical numbers "6", "17", "8", "9" and "11". Thirteen aircraft were from the 6th batch, tactical numbers "16" and "2" (s/nos 1A-06001, 1A-06002), tactical numbers "100", "3", "7", "15", "4", "1", "5" and "12" (s/nos 1A-06005 – 1A-06012), "14" (s/n 1A-06014) and "18" (s/n 1A-06018. In June 1958 the 25. PLM handed over the last six Lim-1 fighters (preserved) to OSL-4 at Dęblin.

Deliveries of Lim-1 aircraft from the 6th batch were directed in October 1953 to the 29. PLM based at Orneta. They allowed equipment of this regiment to also be entirely with Polish-built aircraft. In the first lot on 24 October 1953 the 29.

[79]: Lim-1 "04" (s/n 1A09004) of Piła-based 6. PLSz.

[80]: Lim-1 "04" (s/n 1A-01004) of Orneta-based 29. PLM. This is the second Lim-1 with tactical number "04".

81

[81]: Lim-1 "05" (s/n 1A09005). It was completed in WSK Mielec on 1 April 1954. On 22 April 1954 it entered the inventory of Mierzęcice-based 39. PLM, where it served for three years. Subsequently, during 23 July 1957 – 23 October 1959 it was operated by Piła-based 6. PLM-Sz.

[82]: Lim-1s "18" and "10", of the 2. PLM at Cracow-Rakowice/Czyżyny airfield.

82

83 *[83]: Lim-1 "16" of the 30. PLSz MW, Siemirowice, circa 1958. Previously it was alleged to have the serial number 1A-03004. Note the peeling-off number "16" on the vertical stabilizer.*

[84]: Lim-1s from the 7th production batch, delivered to the 5. DLM in early 1954.

84

85

[85]: Lim-1 "637" (s/n 1A06037) of the 31. PLM, Warsaw Bemowo/ Babice airfield, summer of 1954. 1st Michał Polech is climbing the ladder. The aircraft came from the 6th production batch and sports a three-digit tactical number.

86 *[86]: Lim-1 "24" (s/n1A07008) of the 34. PLM MW, Gdynia-Babie Doły air base, 1954.*

PLM received aircraft with serial numbers 1A-06019 through 1A-06027. Aircraft of the second lot, delivered three weeks later, were also from the 6th batch: s/n 1A-06028, s/n 1A-06036 and s/n 1A-06038. The new fighters replaced the previously operated Yak-23s.

In mid-November 1953 in the inventory of the 34. PLM MW were eight Lim-1 fighters. The ninth Lim-1 on strength at that time, "10" (s/n 1A-03003), was damaged on 11 November. W/O Kazimierz Sobestjański, cleared for his first solo, overshot the "T" mark on landing by about 800 m. The late touchdown meant that the aircraft stopped about 430 m beyond the end of the runway of Gdynia-Babie Doły air base. The aircraft was severely damaged, but returned to service. The pilot was unhurt. During preparations for an air parade in Gdynia on the Navy Day an accident occurred. During a formation training flight on 24 June 1954 two Lim-1 aircraft, flying at about 600 km/h, collided in the air. The aircraft flown by LtJG Zdzisław Ostałowski hit the lead aircraft, flown by LtJG Henryk Wojtecki. Despite damage both pilots managed to regain control and landed safely at their airfield. The aircraft were sent for emergency repairs.

In April 1954 in the inventory of the 34. PLM MW were 19 Lim-1 fighters, with the following tactical and serial numbers (respectively in brackets): "2", "4", "8" and "12" (1A-02001–1A-02004), "6", "10", "14" and "16" (1A-03001–1A-03004), "18" (1A-06040), "40", "20" and "22" (1A-07001–1A- 07003), "36" (1A-07005), "24", "28" and "30" (1A-07008–1A-07010), "32" and "38" (1A-07014–1A-07015) and "34" (1A-07039).

In 1957 the 30. PL MW based at Cewice was reformed into the 30. PLSz MW (*Pułk Lotnictwa Szturmowego Marynarki Wojennej* – Naval Attack Aviation Regiment) and re-equipment of this unit with Lim-1 aircraft began. In late October 1957 from the 34. PLM MW two Lim-1s were transferred to Cewice: "30" (s/n 1A- 07010) and "38" (s/n 1A-07015). In November another two aircraft were transferred: "8" (s/n 1A- 02003) and "2" (1A-02010). In April 1958 there were 19 Lim-1 aircraft in the regiment's inventory.

The Lim-1 aircraft of the 2nd, 3rd and later production batches, as well as aircraft from the 7th batch that entered service in 1953 received (as previously) one- and two-digit tactical numbers,

87

[87]: Lim-1 "24" (s/n 1A07008) collided during taxiing with the Lim-1 "40" standing on the apron on 6 February 1957.

88

[88]: Lim-1 "40" (s/n 1A07001) of the 34. PLM after the aforementioned collision. Note the tactical numbers not related to the serial numbers.

89 *[89]: Lim-1s of the 34. PLM MW at Siemirowice air base in 1958. On the first three aircraft the following numbers are visible: "26" (s/n 1A07 007), "14" (s/n 1A03003) and "22" (s/n 1A07003).*

[90]: *Lim-1 "36" (s/n 1A-07005) of the 34. PLM MW in flight near the Bay of Gdańsk.*

[91]: *Lim-1 "712" (s/n 1A07012) first served in the 31. PLM. This air-to-air photograph was taken during its service in OSL-4 at Dęblin with an instructor, 1st Lt Andrzej Majewski, at the controls. Dęblin, summer of 1958.*

92]: *Lim-1 "724" (s/n 1A07024) on display in Warsaw in 1957. This aircraft entered service in December 1953 in a regiment of the 5. DLM. It was lost in a crash in Dęblin-based 58. LPSz-B on 24 June 1964.*

[93]: Lim-1 "736" (s/n 1A07036) of the 1. PLM. It was lost in a crash on 18 August 1954.

[94]: Lim-1 "88" (s/n 1A08008) of Malbork-based 41. PLM. (The eighth aircraft of the eighth production batch, with two-digit tactical number). The number 88 is repeated on the expended case container. From April 1958 it was in the inventory of the 59. PSz-B at Biała Podlaska.

not related to the serial number. Tactical numbers of Lim-1 aircraft were repeated among aircraft that were in inventories of various units. Following aircraft on strength of the 25. PLM in 1954 may serve as an example: (s/n 1A-06002) had the tactical number "2", (s/n 1A-05008) – "8", (s/n 1A-06012) – "12", (s/n 1A-05006) – "6", (s/n 1A-06014) – "14", (s/n 1A-06001) – "16", (s/n 1A-06018) – "18" and (s/n 1A- 06004) – "20". In 1954 in the inventory of the 25. PLM there were 17 Lim-1 aircraft in two squadrons and one (s/n 1A-06005) tactical number "100" in the staff flight. After deliveries of Lim-2 aircraft in 1955 the twelve Lim-1s still operating were dispersed among the regiment's squadrons. Ten were assigned to the 3rd Squadron and one each was assigned to the 1st and 2nd Squadron. The 25. PLM ceased Lim-1 operations in mid-June 1958 and the last six aircraft of this type were transferred to OSL-4 in Dęblin.

The Lim-1 aircraft assembled in the first quarter of 1954 were intended for the 5. DLM. Older MiG-15 fighters from three regiments of this division were transferred to other units. Three regiments of the 5. DLM, 1. PLM, 13. PLM and 31. PLM, received 37 aircraft of the 7th production batch, numbering 60 aircraft. Aircraft of the 7th batch that entered service in 1954 received three-digit tactical numbers, related to the serial number. The following serial numbers and tactical numbers related to them (in brackets) of 10 Lim-1 aircraft delivered to the 1. PLM on 18 January may serve as an example: "711" (s/n 1A-07011), "713" (s/n 1A-07013), "716" (s/n 1A-07016), "718" (s/n 1A-07018), "720" (s/n 1A-07020), "722" (s/n 1A-07022), "723" (s/n 1A-07023), "726" (s/n 1A-07026), "727" (s/n 1A-07027) and "733" (s/n 1A-07033), as well as the next four: "731" (s/n 1A-07031), "736" (s/n 1A-07036), "746" (s/n 1A-07046) and "747" (s/n 1A-07047), which entered inventory of this regiment on 18 February 1954.

Eleven Lim-1 aircraft of the 7th production batch were delivered to the 13. PLM, based at Leźnica Wielka near Łęczyca. The 31. PLM, still based at Warsaw Bemowo/Babice, received 13 aircraft of the same batch. In the 13. PLM the first Lim-1 crash occurred on 27 April 1954. 2nd Lt Bronisław Drobnik took off for a basic and intermediate flying training sortie at 5,000 m. He probably lost consciousness and the aircraft went into spin, crashing off Borszyn near Leźnica Wielka and burning. The pilot was killed. The second crash of a Lim-1 took place on the next day in the 1. PLM, based at Warsaw Bemowo/Babice airfield. On 28 April the engine of the Lim-1 "723" (s/n 1A 07023) cut out in flight. The pilot, 2nd Lt Ignacy Dobras, decided to land at the departure airfield instead of bailing out. However, the aircraft stalled and crashed into a Warsaw residential building, killing the pilot. The crash was caused by an engine failure.

During the first three months of 1954 assembly of Lim-1 aircraft intended for the regiments of the 5. DLM, which transferred older MiG-15s to other units, was going on. Two regiments, 1. PLM and 31. PLM, received 13 aircraft each, while the 13. PLM received 11 new aircraft.

From April 1954 on the new Lim-1 aircraft were delivered to units based in northern Poland. Eight Lim-1 aircraft from the 8th production batch, accepted by the military inspection, were assigned to Słupsk-based 28. PLM, and aircraft (s/n 1A-08015) was assigned to the staff flight of the 10. DLM headquarters. Of the next batch of 10 Lim-1 aircraft, completed in mid-June 1954, the 28. PLM received seven.

The Lim-1 were demonstrated publicly for the first time in flight on 22 July 1954, during an air parade over Lublin. Formations of five three-ship flights each came from the 1. PLM, 13. PLM, 31. PLM and 39. PLM. In the next month, on 18 July a second Lim-1 crash in the 1. PLM took place. The regiment's pilots were flying group sorties that day. During the manoeuvre of formation disassembly before landing the Lim-1 "736" (s/n 1A-07036), flown by 2nd Lt Aleksander Dunal, collided with the aircraft flown by his wingman, 1st Lt Ryszard Grundman. The Lim-1 "736", damaged during the collision, descended rapidly and crashed near the village of Truskaw off Mińsk Mazowiecki. The bailout attempt failed and the pilot was killed. 1st Lt Grundman landed safely.

In April and May 1954 eighteen Lim-1 aircraft from the 8th, 9th and 10th production batch were delivered to the 39. PLM based at Mierzęcice. On 27 July 1954 the fourth crash of a Lim-1 took place in the 39. PLM. It was caused by an engine failure of the Lim-1 "07" (s/n 1A-09007) during a night flight in good weather conditions. Forced landing near the villages of Ożarowice and Brynica ended in crash. The pilot, 2nd Lt Stanisław Abramek was killed. The next emergency landing in the 39. PLM on 11 March 1955 ended happily. 2nd Lt Kazimierz Ciapała made a belly landing in the Lim-1 "19" (s/n 1A-08019) off Przyszowice near Gliwice.

On 10 August 1954 the 21st Independent Reconnaissance Aviation Regiment (21. *Samodzielny Pułk Lotnictwa Rozpoznawczego* – 21. SPLR) based at Sochaczew received 8 Lim-1 aircraft: (s/nos 1A-10004, 1A-10 005, 1A-10006, 1A-10008, 1A-10014, 1A-11010, 1A-11013 and 1A-11016). These aircraft had no reconnaissance equipment and were used for visual reconnaissance training.

In 1954 four Lim-1 aircraft, "01" (s/n 1A-11001), "07" (s/n 1A-11007), "09" (s/n 1A-11009) and "11" (s/n 1A-11011), were assigned to the 19. LEH 19th (*Lotnicza Eskadra Holownicza* – Target Tow Squadron), based at Świdwin. They were operated

[95]: Lim-1 "19" (s/n 1A-08019) from Mierzęcice-based 39. PLM after a successful emergency landing by 2nd Lt Kazimierz Ciapała in Przyszowice near Gliwice on 11 March 1955.

[96]: Lim-1 "904" (s/n 1A-09004) from OSL-4 at Dęblin. Initially it had the tactical number "04".

[97]: Lim-1 "09" (s/n 1A10009). The motorcycle is a WFM M06, 19 LEH, Świdwin, 1956.

by the 19. LEH until September 1958 and then transferred to the 61. LPSz-B based at Nowe Miasto.

On 27 September 1954 the 2. PLM, based at Cracow received factory-fresh Lim-1 aircraft from the 11th and 12th production batches.

On 10 October 1954 the first Lim-1 aircraft were delivered to Krzesiny air base. It was the first delivery of factory-fresh aircraft to the 11. PLM, based there. Among the delivered aircraft were (s/nos 1A-11019, 1A-11020, 1A-12001, 1A-12003, 1A-12004, 1A-12005, 1A-12006, 1A-12008 and 1A-12010). These aircraft received tactical numbers in form of the two last digits of the serial number, respectively "19", "20", "01", "03", "04", "05", "06", "08" and "10". They were assigned to the 3rd Squadron of the 11. PLM. They were redeployed in two five-aircraft lots on 25 and 26 October 1954 from Krzesiny to the newly-built Debrzno air base. The Lim-1s, delivered to the 11. PLM in the second, later, lot were transferred from other units. Only their tactical numbers are known: "101", "110", "114", "117", "120", "121", "122", "134", "161", "171", "191" and "199". There are no serial numbers of these aircraft in the regiment's documents.

In 1955 four Lim-1 crashes took place. The first occurred on 28 January in the 13. PLM. 2nd Lt Józef Górka lost his flight leader's aircraft from sight during a cross-country sortie in a two-ship formation. During the attempt to land off-airport with the undercarriage deployed the aircraft crashed near the village of Skowron, near Pińczów. The pilot was killed.

The second tragedy took place on 1 April in Słupsk-based 28. PLM. 2nd Lt Antoni Łabądź, having completed a medium flying training sortie, made a steep turn over the runway during a high-speed approach, causing the aircraft to go into spin. The Lim-1 crashed 500 m from the border of the Słupsk air base. The pilot was killed. The third crash in 1955 took place in Orneta-based 29. PLM. 1st Lt Sylwester Konik, flying as a wingman of Maj. Adam Buczyński, lost him from sight. Looking for him, he was circling and stalled the aircraft, which went into spin and crashed into Bianki lake. The sunken aircraft was Lim-1 "20" (s/n 1A-00620). 1st Lt Konik did not fall into the lake with the aircraft, as was stated in the post-accident report. He ejected, but the wind pushed him away from the crash site. Landing in a field, he broke both legs and could not walk. He was found dead in the summer and only then was the order of the Air Force commander about this tragedy published.

On 18 June 1955 in Debrzno-based 11. PLM a crash took place during a practice dogfight at low altitude. 2nd Lt Tadeusz Sołtysiak, piloting the Lim-1 "19" (s/n 1A-11019), was killed. His aircraft crashed near the village of Stare Gronowo. In 1956, after the arrival of the first lot of Lim-2 aircraft, the 11. PLM began to transfer older Lim-1s to attack units.

In October 1956 a selected group of pilots from Bydgoszcz-based 5. PLSz commenced conversion to jet-powered aircraft. As early as December 1956 the first Lim-1 arrived in the unit. It was the beginning of the end of Il-10 attack aircraft service in the Bydgoszcz-based regiment, which in June 1959 became the 5. PLSz.

In 1956 there were no Lim-1 crashes, but three occurred in 1957. The first one took place on 30 January 1957 in the 1st Training Squadron of the 58. PSz-B of OSL-4 at Dęblin during a medium flying training sortie. 1st Lt Stefan Łazarek was killed, making risky manoeuvres at dangerously low altitude. His Lim-1 "749" crashed in inverted flight. The second crash took place on 28 March 1958 in the 1st Training Squadron at Nowe Miasto. A student of Radom-based No. OSL-5, Pvt Officer Cadet Władysław Wojciechowski, caused the Lim-1 aircraft to go into spin when practising loops and could not recover. The aircraft crashed near Kłopoczyn, killing the pilot. The third crash also occurred in a training unit. It took place on 19 July 1957, again in the 1st Training Squadron of the 58. PSz-B of

[98]: *Veterans of the Polish Air Force converting to jet aircraft in the 62. PSz-T LM based at Poznań-Krzesiny pose next to the Lim-1 "803". Left to right: Maj. Ignacy Olszewski, unknown, unknown, Maj. Wacław Król and Maj. Witold Łokuciewski.*

[99]: *Lim-1 "803" of the 62. PSz-T LM. Standing in front of the aircraft are, left to right, Maj. Ignacy Olszewski, Maj. Witold Łokuciewski, unkown, unknown, Maj. Wacław Król. Krzesiny, 1956.*

OSL-4 at Dęblin. It was more tragic than the previous one. During a two-ship formation flight the Lim-1 of Pvt. Officer Cadet Tadeusz Libuda, who was flying his first solo formation sortie, collided with the Lim-2 aircraft of the instructor, Capt. Aleksander Sroka, over the village of Uściąż near Kazimierz Dolny. Both pilots were killed and one Lim-1 and one Lim-2 aircraft were lost.

The 30. PLSz MW based at Siemirowice (Cewice) received Lim-1 aircraft in 1957. In October "30" (s/n 1A- 07010) and "38" (s/n 1A-07015) and in November "8" (s/n 1A-02003) and "2" (s/n 1A-02001) were transferred from the 34. PLM MW. In August 1957 the 30. PLSz MW received their first Lim-2 aircraft.

In late January 1958 formation of the 59. PSz-B of "Janek Krasicki" Officer Flying Training School began at Biała Podlaska airfield. In April the first lot of nine Lim-1 aircraft was transferred from Malbork-based 41. PLM: (s/nos 1A-08002, 1A-08004, 1A-08005, 1A-08008, 1A-08011, 1A-10005, 1A-10015, 1A-10018 and 1A-10020). On 2 July four older Lim-1 fighters were transferred from Orneta-based 29. PLM: (s/nos 1A-06028, 1A-06029, 1A-06033 and 1A-06034). On 1 December 1959 in the inventory of the 59. PSz-B and its squadrons were 74 aircraft of various types. Among 33 combat aircraft there were 16 Lim-1 aircraft: (s/nos 1A-01003, 1A-06011, 1A-06021, 1A- 06028, 1A-06033, 1A-07055, 1A-08002, 1A-08004, 1A-08005, 1A-08008, 1A-08011, 1A-10005, 1A-10015, 1A-10018 and 1A-10020). From spring of 1958 several dozen officer cadets per year were trained at Biała Podlaska.

In 1959 two Lim-1 crashes in combat training regiments took place. The first occurred on 19 March in the 60th Combat Training Regiment of the "Żwirko and Wigura" Officer Flying Training School at Radom. 1st Lt Marian Suliga went into spin and did not recover. The aircraft crashed near the village of Wierzbica, near Radom, killing the pilot.

On 3 June 1959 a crash in the Biała Podlaska-based 59. PSz-B occurred. The Lim-1 "755" (s/n 1A-07055) had an engine failure during a practice ground target strafing sortie at Jagodne firing range near Łuków. The pilot, Sgt. Officer Cadet Bogdan Pawłowski, made an emergency landing attempt, but the aircraft crashed and the pilot was killed. In the early 1960s the training units of both officer flying training schools were also involved in exercises. In the autumn of 1960 Lim-1s of the 59. PSz-B took part in an exercise organized at the highest level, codenamed "*Burza*" (Storm). The combat component was redeployed to a provisional grass airfield as Wysokie Mazowieckie. Several trees in the forest were cut down to make approach easier. In 1961 training of the fourth group of officer cadets of the 3rd year began at Biała Podlaska. The most intense flight training period lasted from May to July.

On 10 June 1961 the Lim-1 "707" (s/n 1A-07007) was damaged, when an officer cadet made a belly landing at Radom. The aircraft was repaired and returned to service. Two months later, on 10 August, another crash took place at Biała Podlaska. 1st Lt Włodzimierz Wierzba was killed when flying the Lim-1 "101" (s/n 1A-01001). On approach to land he did not make the base turn. The aircraft suddenly went into steep dive and crashed near the village of Sławacinek. On 9 May 1963 in the 59. PSz-B the Lim-1 "118" (s/n 1A-10018) was lost in a crash with the pilot. Two minutes after take-off from Biała Podlaska airfield the aircraft, with landing gear still lowered, went into spin, crashed and exploded 5 km away from the airfield. The pilot, PFC Officer Cadet Jan Dziekoński, was killed. The cause of the crash was not discovered. After a week of recess in flying the flight training was resumed. In June 1963 four Lim-1 aircraft arrived at the regiment from the 61. PSz-B, based at Nowe Miasto nad Pilicą. These were: (s/nos 1A-08036, 1A-07029, 1A-08002, 1A-08003, 1A-08008, 1A-08009, 1A-10009, 1A-10015, 1A-11008, 1A-11016 and1A-12007). Several Lim-1 fighters were sent to No. 2 Military Aircraft Repair Works in Bydgoszcz for conversion to SBLim-1 two-seat combat trainers.

In the early 1960s the Lim-1 aircraft were still operated by the 58. PSz-B, based at Dęblin. On 18 January 1961 "711" (s/n 1A-07011) was lost due to a failure. After completing several aerobatic figures at the altitude of 4,000 m, the aircraft ceased to react to control stick movements. The instructor pilot, 2nd Lt Jan Karpiński, ejected safely. On 22 May 1962 during a practice two-ship formation flight the Lim-1 s/n 1A-02003, flown by Officer Cadet Jan Wielgolewski, collided with the Lim-2 "1127" (s/n 1B-01127) flown by the instructor. The damaged Lim-1, which had lost its vertical stabilizer, went into a spin and crashed near Żelechów, killing the pilot. The instructor, 2nd Lt Aleksander Turczyniak, managed to nurse the damaged Lim-2 "1127" to Dęblin airfield. The Lim-1 (s/n 1A-02003) had been previously operated by the 34. PLM MW and 30. PLSz MW with tactical number "8". The last Lim-1 crash in Dęblin-based 58. PSz-B took place on 24 June 1964. When Sgt Officer Cadet Aleksander Fudała was returning from a practice gun camera ground target strafing sortie at Jagodne bombing range the engine cut out at an altitude of 800 m. The pilot did not eject, but decided to make an emergency landing instead. The Lim-1 "724" (s/n 1A-07024) hit a tree and crashed in the village of Soćki near Stoczek Łukowski. The ejection seat worked and ejected the pilot from the exploding aircraft. Officer Cadet Fudała sustained severe injuries and died on the way to hospital.

The in-flight engine flameout of Lim-1 "120" (s/n 1A-10020) of the 61. PSz-B, based at Nowe Miasto near Pilicą led to the loss of the aircraft on 18 August 1964. The engine cut out at an altitude of 10,000 m. Three restart attempts, made at the altitudes of 9,000, 7,000 and 3,000 m, failed and Cpl Officer Cadet Eugeniusz Prokopowicz bailed out at 2,100 m and his Lim-1 crashed near Chęciny.

The number of Lim-1 aircraft built by WSK Mielec factory given in various publications varies from 227 to 231. Five pre-production aircraft with serial numbers 1A-01001 through 1A-01005, assembled from Soviet-made components, together with aircraft of 12 production batches give a total number of 233 Lim-1 aircraft built, according to Grzegorz Klimasiński's research.

Serial numbers of Lim-1 aircraft, built in 12 production batches: (s/nos 1A-01001–1A-01005), (s/nos 1A-02001–1A-02005), (s/nos 1A-03001–1A-03005), (s/nos 1A-04001–1A-04008), (s/nos 1A-05001–1A-05010), (s/nos 1A-06001–1A-06040), (s/nos 1A-07001–1A-07060), (s/nos 1A-08001–1A-08020), (s/nos 1A-09001–1A-09020), (s/nos 1A-10001–1A-10020), (s/nos 1A-11001–1A-11020), (s/nos 1A-12001–1A-12020).

Eighteen Lim-1 aircraft were lost in crashes and two due to failures.

100 *[100]: Lim-1 "21" with unknown serial number. With identical tactical number "21" the MiG-15 (s/n 20135) was operated by the 28. PLM based at Słupsk and 25. PLM, based at Pruszcz Gdański.*

[101]: Lim-1 “8” (s/n 1A02003) was one of two first jet-powered fighters delivered to the 34. PLM MW, Gdynia-Babie Doły air base, April 1953. The duraluminum skin with varying sheen on individual panels is covered with transparent lacquer coating. The fin tip is red.

101

[102]: Lim-1 “8” (s/n 1A02003) of the 34. PLM MW, Gdynia-Babie Doły air base, second half of the 1950s. The serial number is visible in the “waist” of the digit “8”.

102

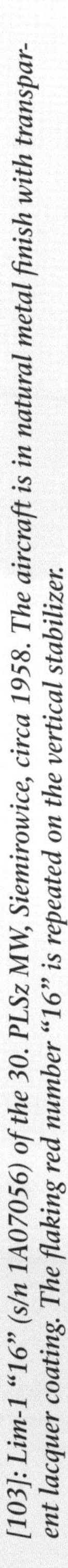

103

[103]: *Lim-1 "16" (s/n 1A07056) of the 30. PLSz MW, Siemirowice, circa 1958. The aircraft is in natural metal finish with transparent lacquer coating. The flaking red number "16" is repeated on the vertical stabilizer.*

104

[104]: *Lim-1 "16" (s/n 1A07056) of the 30. PLSz MW, Siemirowice, circa 1958. Previously the serial number 1A-03004 was erroneously reported for this aircraft. Note the flaking number "16" on the vertical stabilizer.*

105

[105]: Lim-1 “10” (s/n 1A11010) of the 21. SPLRT, Sochaczew 1955. The aircraft is modified for aerial target towing.

106

[106]: Lim-1 “10” (s/n 1A11010) of the 21. SPLRT, modified for target drogue towing. The towing line hook is mounted under the lower forward fuselage section. One 23 mm cannon had been removed.

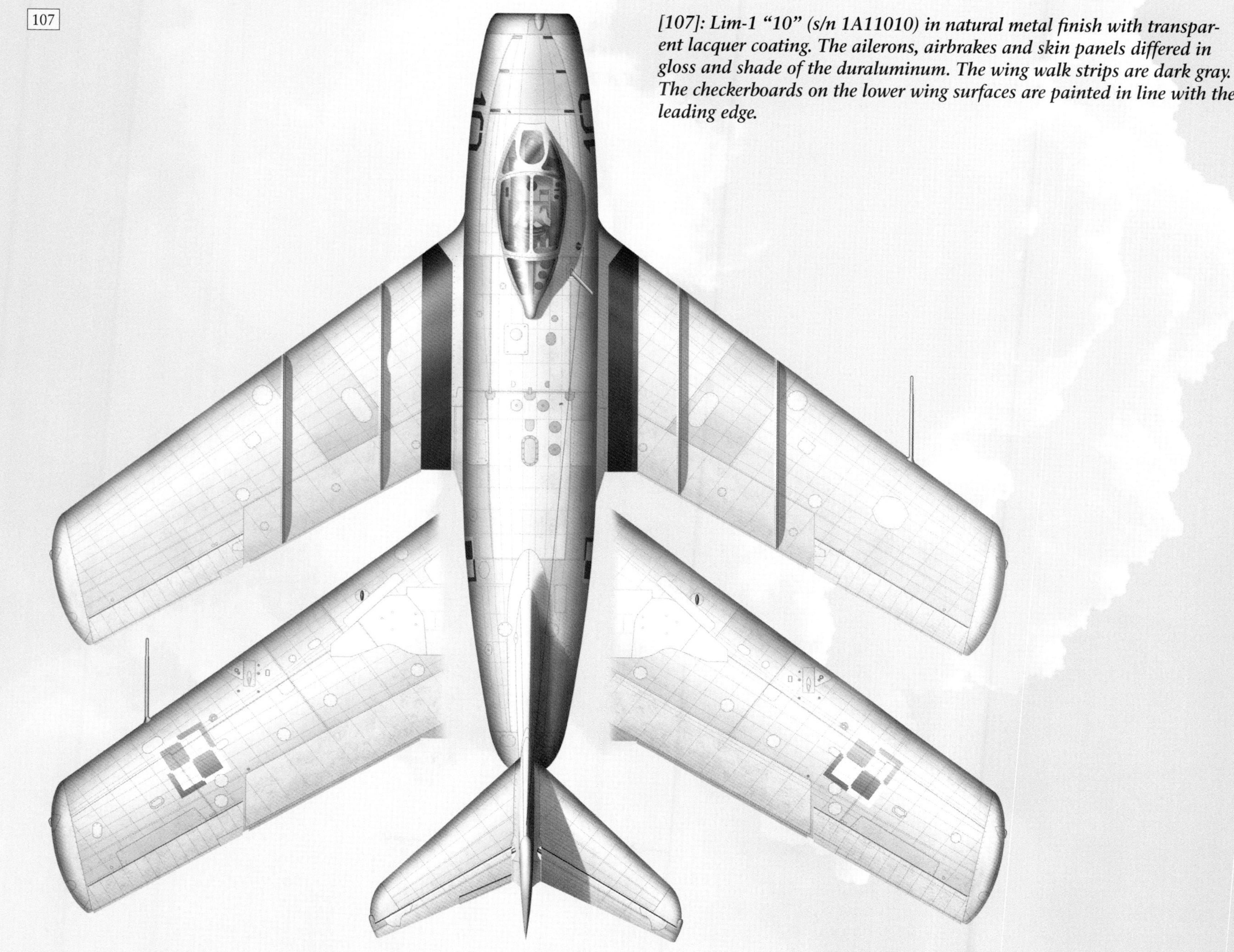

[107]: Lim-1 “10” (s/n 1A11010) in natural metal finish with transparent lacquer coating. The ailerons, airbrakes and skin panels differed in gloss and shade of the duraluminum. The wing walk strips are dark gray. The checkerboards on the lower wing surfaces are painted in line with the leading edge.

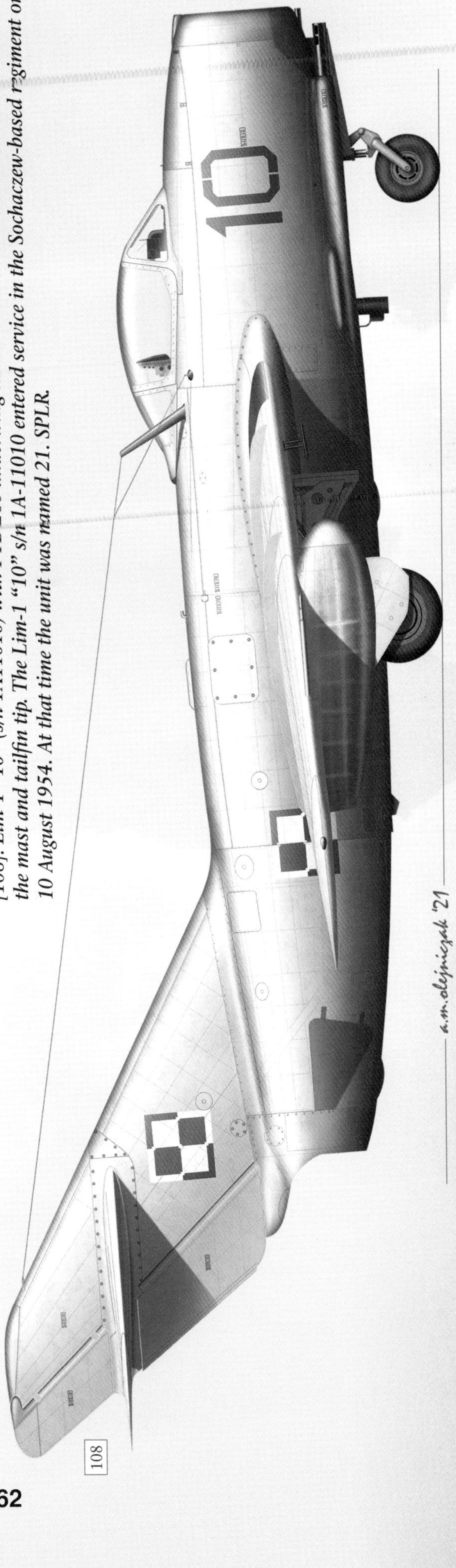

108

[108]: Lim-1 "10" (s/n 1A11010) with PTB 260 underwing tanks. The wire antenna is stretched between the mast and tailfin tip. The Lim-1 "10" s/n 1A-11010 entered service in the Sochaczew-based regiment on 10 August 1954. At that time the unit was named 21. SPLR.

a.m.olejniczak '21

109

[109]: Lim-1 "10" (s/n 1A11010) of the 21. SPLR.

[110]: Lim-1 "104" (s/n 1A12004) of the 4. PLM, Goleniów 1958. The aircraft is in natural metal finish with transparent lacquer coating and green tailfin tip. The serial number is visible in the digit 4 of the tactical number.

[111+112]: Lim-1 "104" (s/n 1A12004) from the 12th (last) production batch in the 4. PLM based at Goleniów in 1958. It was previously operated by Debrzno-based 11. PLM with the tactical number "04".

Lim-1.5

In the WSK an upgrade of the Lim-1 radio equipment, to align it with that of the Lim-2, was developed. The concept was accepted by the Air Force headquarters. The upgrade was to be done during planned overhauls at the Military Aircraft Repair Works. Modified Lim-1s with radio equipment unified with that of the Lim-2 were unofficially referred to as Lim-1.5. The RSI-6K wireless set was replaced with the R-800V VHF transceiver. The RPKO-10M direction finder was replaced by an ARK-5 ADF. Additionally, an MRP-8E beacon signal receiver of the instrument landing system was added. The RV-2 radar altimeter and SRU-0 IFF were also added. In the latter half of the 1950s several dozen Lim-1 aircraft were upgraded to this standard.

[113]: Lim-1.5 "21". In the mid-1950s several Lim-1 fighters were upgraded. During the overhauls they were fitted with more advanced avionics and received the unofficial designation Lim-1.5.

Lim-2 (1B)

The Lim-2 was initially referred to as "product CD", from the Russian designation "product SD". It was a MiG-15bis built under license in Poland, and received the factory designation 1B. The first Lim-2, built by WSK Mielec on 17 September 1954, had the serial number 1B-00101. Nineteen production batches were planned. It was assumed that the first four batches would number 20 aircraft each and the rest would be larger, with 30 aircraft in each. Along with the start of the Lim-2 production the WSK Rzeszów factory launched licence production of VK-1A engines, with the TBO increased from 200 to 250 hours. The Rzeszów-built engines were designated Lis-2 (abbreviation of "*licencyjny silnik drugi*", licence engine two). In the first 100 Lim-2s Soviet-built VK-1A engines were installed. From the 101st aircraft, s/n 1B-006 02 completed on 24 February 1955, Polish Lis-2 engines were installed. Production of Lim-2 aircraft enabled replacement of Yak-23 fighters with lesser combat capabilities and weary MiG-15s in fighter aviation regiments. In the Air Defence fighter aviation regiments the first squadrons were gradually equipped with the new Lim-2s. The second squadrons were equipped with older Lim-1s. The third squadrons performed training duties, operating the oldest MiG-15bis and S-102 fighters.

The first Lim-2 aircraft entered service in November and December 1954 in the 5. DLM OPL. Several examples from the 1st and 3rd batches were assigned at that time to the 1. PLM. Among the first delivered were tactical (serial numbers) "103" (s/n 1B-00103), "104" (s/n 1B-00104), "105" (s/n 1B-00105), "315" (s/n 1B-00315), "317" (s/n 1B-00317) and "319" (s/n 1B-00319). In March 1955 "609" (s/n 1B-00609) was delivered to the 1. PLM and in June "825" (s/n 1B-00825) and "901" (s/n 1B-00901).

[114]: Lim-2 "001" with atypical tactical number and unknown serial number.

[115]: Lim-2 "106" (s/n 1B-01006) of the 34. PLM MW. Sitting in the cockpit is Lt Zdzisław Ostałowski. Gdynia-Babie Doły air base, 1958.

116 *[116]: Lim-2 "107" (s/n 1B-01007) of the 34. PLM MW, modified for target drogue towing.*

The next batch of 10 Lim-2s entered the inventory of the 1. PLM on 9 August 1955. These were nine aircraft from the 9th production batch and one from the 10th batch: "902" (s/n 1B-00902), "904" (s/n 1B-00904), "911" (s/n 1B-00911), "912" (s/n 1B-00912), "913" (s/n 1B -00913), "914" (s/n 1B-00914), "918" (s/n 1B-00918), "921" (s/n 1B-00921), "927" (s/n 1B-00927) and "1001" (s/n 1B-01001).

In the latter half of August ten aircraft from the 10th production batch were delivered, with the following tactical numbers: "1004", "1008", "1012", "1013", "1018", "1021, "1022", "1025", "1026" and "1030". On 13 August 1956 the 1. PLM received the final lot of factory-new Lim-2s. These were aircraft from the last (18th and 19th) production batches. In 1956 an aerobatic team on three Lim-2 aircraft was formed in the 1. PLM. The pilots were Captains Zygmunt Dębowski, Jerzy Figurski and Ryszard Grundman. During the Aviation Day display on 26 August 1956 the team performed a spectacular aerobatic routine, including a spectacular group aileron roll. On 24 July 1958 the Lim-2 "1030" (s/n 1B-01030) was lost during a target towing sortie. The pilot flew into a cloud, lost speed and stalled. The pilot ejected successfully and the aircraft crashed in a spin. On 10 March 1959 a fatal crash at the base of the 1. PLM at Mińsk Mazowiecki took place. The Lim-2 "914", piloted by 2nd Lt Jerzy Kowalczuk, caught fire immediately after take-off. The aircraft lost altitude, crashed and exploded, killing the pilot. Five years later, on 9 April 1964 another fatal crash occurred during night training sorties. The pilot probably lost spatial orientation. Only 2.5 minutes after take-off the Lim-2 "418" (s/n 1B-00418) crashed in the village of Prusy near Mińsk Mazowiecki. 2nd Lt Jerzy Szymański was killed. The next year on 3 June the third Lim-2 crash in the 1. PLM took place. During a mock attack on an anti-aircraft gun battery near Warsaw Bemowo/Babice airfield, the Lim-2 "1830" (s/n 1B-01830) crashed during recovery from a dive on the target. The pilot, 1st Lt Robert Chełmiński, sustained severe injuries and died in hospital. Thanks to the deliveries of factory-new Lim-2s from the WSK Mielec factory and rotation of aircraft from other units, during 1954–1965 the 1. PLM operated about 60 of these aircraft. The weary Lim-2 aircraft were struck off the 1. PLM inventory in late 1965.

117

[117]: Lim-2 "307" (s/n 1B-00307) was a personal aircraft of Gen. Jan Frey-Bielecki. Later it was flown by Jan Raczkowski. The expended case container with repeated number "307" is visible.

[118]: Lim-2 "216" (s/n 1B-01216) with expended case container, carrying a bomb under the port wing.

118

119

[119]: Lim-2 "317" (s/n 1B-00317) with expended case container. Note the characteristic shape of the tactical number digits.

[121]: Lim-2 "415" (s/n 1B-00415) of the 5.PLM-Sz based at Bydgoszcz. It was converted to the Lim-2R variant in 1964 and lost in a crash with the Sochaczew-based 32. PLRTiA on 10 July 1970.

120

[120]: Lim-2 "420" (s/n 1B004-20) of the 9. PLM based at Debrzno.

121

[122]: The Lim-2s "501" (s/n 1B-005-01) and "509" (s/n 1B-00509) were delivered to the 25. PLM in the winter of 1955. In July 1956 and December 1957 both aircraft were in the inventory of Debrzno-based 11. PLM. This photograph was first published in the "Świat" (World) weekly in 1958.

122

[123]: Lim-2 (s/n 1B-00501) damaged after hitting trees on approach to landing during service with the 28. PLM. The digit "0" was added in the tactical number, because a Lim-5 in the regiment's inventory also had the number 501. Słupsk-Redzikowo air base, March 1964.

In mid-November 1954 Lim-2s began to enter service in the Słupsk-based 10. DLM. On 22 January 1955 eight Lim-2 aircraft from the 4th and 5th production batches entered the inventory of the 25. PLM, based at Pruszcz Gdański. These had following tactical numbers: "414", "416", "417", "418", "420", "501", "509" and "511". In March and April eight Lim-2s from the 6th and 7th batches were delivered to the 25. PLM. In August the regiment received ten Lim-2s from the 10th batch. On 9 August 1955 on strength of the 25. PLM were 23 Lim-2 fighters with following tactical numbers: "414", "416", "417", "418", "420", "501", "509", "511", "620", "701", "705", "707", "713", "1002", "1003", "1005", "1006", "1007", "1009", "1010", "1011", "1014" and "1019" (and 12 Lim-1s still in service).

[124]: Lim-2 "0501" (s/n 1B00-501) of the 21. PLR. The serial number 1B00-501 is erroneously painted on the gun fairing and nosewheel bay door. The atypical tactical number "0501" was retained after the overhaul.

124

125

[125]: Lim-2s "714" and "716" of Malbork-based 41. PLM in 1960. "714" was lost in a crash in the 28. PLM on 2 December 1964.

126

[126]: Maj. Stanisław Skalski standing next to the Lim-2 "518". The photo was taken during his conversion course to jet aircraft in the 62. PSz-T LM based at Poznań-Krzesiny in 1957.

[127]: Lim-2 "518" (s/n 1B005-18) of the 62. PSz-T LM. Standing in front of the aircraft is a flight instructor, 1st Lt Telesfor Krukowski. Krzesiny air base, 1956.

[128]: Lim-2s "820" and "1630" of the 10. PLM.

[129]: Lim-2 "822" (s/n 1B-00822) of Łask-based 10. PLM at Cracow-Balice airfield. For the duration of the exercise in 1961 the aircraft had a white stripe painted around the fuselage.

[130]: Lim-2 "825" (s/n 1B-00825) delivered on 3 June 1955 to the 1. PLM Warsaw, from where it was transferred to Babimost-based 45. PLM on 27 January 1958.

[131]: Lim-2 "825" (s/n 1B008-25) during service in the 3. PLM, photographed at Wrocław-Strachowice air base.

In 1956 new Lim-2 aircraft from the 13th, 14th, 17th and 18th batches entered the regiment's inventory. Older Lim-2s from the 4th through 7th batches were transferred to the 11. PLM in early 1956.

When ten new Lim-5 fighters entered the inventory of the regiment, a rotation of aircraft was made. By May 1957 the oldest Lim-2s from the 4th and 10th batches were transferred to the 26. PLM, 29. PLM and 38. PLM. After this rotation, on 1 December 1957 in the inventory of the 25. PLM were 26 Lim-2 aircraft from the 12th, 13th, 14th, 17th and 18th batches. During the airshow on Aviation Day on 8 September 1957 a group flypast of 25 Lim-2 aircraft in parade formation of five five-ship flights was demonstrated over the Bemowo/Babice airfield. Due to shortage of groundcrews in the 25. PLM eight Lim-2 aircraft were put in storage in November 1957. During a formation flight at an altitude of 10,000 m on 25 August 1958 a failure of Lim-2 "1721" occurred. 2nd Lt Aleksander Dmitruk felt a jolt, after which the aircraft ceased to react to flight control inputs and began to bank to starboard. The pilot ejected successfully and the aircraft crashed near the town of Łobez. In September 1958 there were 19 Lim-2 aircraft in the regiment's inventory. On 8 April 1959 during an aerial target interception sortie an engine failure in Lim-2 "1328" occurred. 2nd Lt Jan Mikulski ejected near Drzewiany off Zegrze Pomorskie, but had not fastened the leg strap of the parachute harness. After the separation of the seat and deployment of the parachute he slipped out of the harness and was killed. On the same day 1st Lt Tadeusz Kalinowski observed malfunction of the engine and made an emergency landing at the Zegrze air base. Pilots of Lim-2 and Lim-5 aircraft took part in the parade and air show over the Decade Stadium in Warsaw during the central harvest festival on 6 September 1959. In October 1959 in the regiment's inventory were as many as 11 Lim-5 aircraft. Among the 19 Lim-2 aircraft still in service there were one example each of the 2nd, 5th and 7th batches. The remaining aircraft were from the 13th, 17th and 18th batches. The second Lim-2 crash in the 25. PLM took place on 25 February 1960.

1st Lt Henryk Gnacikowski, flying Lim-2 "1733" on an UTI MiG-15 practice night interception sortie in bad weather conditions, probably fainted after 2 -3 minutes of flight. He was killed

131

[132]: Lim-2s "902", "927", "1012" and "1018" delivered from the WSK factory to the 1. PLM in August 1955, photographed before the 1st Fighter Aviation Contest at Wrocław-Strachowice air base in September 1959. The Lim-2 "1012" was lost in a crash in 1962, when serving in the 25. PLM, based at Pruszcz Gdański.

132

in unclear circumstances in the aircraft, that crashed near the village of Kozielec off Grudziądz. In late May 1960 there were 17 Lim-2 aircraft in the regiment's inventory, but in August five Lim-2s were transferred to the 3. PLM. From May to late September 1960 the 25. PLM was based at Szymany airfield near Szczytno. On the 550th anniversary of the victorious battle an air parade over the fields of Grunwald was organized. On that occasion the famous "plate" formation of 64 Lim-2 and Lim-5 fighters was displayed. The pilots of the 25. PLM were flying a 16-ship box of 8 Lim-2 and 8 Lim-5 aircraft on the right side of the formation. In 1961 as result of aircraft rotation the regiment received three Lim-2 aircraft from the 1. PLM "Warsaw". The third Lim-2 crash in the 25. PLM took place during day training sorties in bad weather conditions. Due to a technical failure the Lim-2 "1012" lost height with a wing dropped and crashed three minutes after take-off near Mierzeszyn, 28 km away from the base. The pilot, 2nd Lt Lech Skirmunt, was killed. In May 1963 the 25. PLM received two Lim-2 aircraft from Łask-based 31. PSz-B. One of these aircraft, "1510", force landed on the grass part of the airfield with the landing gear retracted because the pilot was not able to lower the right landing gear. The wheels-up landing was successful, the pilot sustained no injuries. The aircraft was repaired and returned to service. The fourth Lim-2 crash in the 25. PLM took place on 9 March 1964 during a night flight in bad weather conditions. The Lim-2 "1403" crashed 8 km away from the base in the village of Cedry Wielkie and the pilot, 1st Lt Józef Zięba, was killed. As result of aircraft rotation in 1964 three Lim-2 aircraft were taken from the 30. PLM-Sz MW and three other were transferred to the 11. PLM OPK. During a training redeployment to Wdzydze airfield on 31 August 1965 the Lim-2 "1427" was damaged. After touchdown the tyre blew and the aircraft rolled off the runway. It ran onto a railway siding, breaking off the landing gear and ripping out the underwing fuel tanks from their pylons. The damage was repaired and the aircraft returned to service. In September there were only nine Lim-2 aircraft in the regiment's inventory and in December eight were transferred from the 1. PLM "Warsaw". On the turn of 1967/68, when the regiment was being disbanded, several Lim-2 aircraft were transferred to Debrzno-based 9. PLM and the remaining examples went to the training regiments.

The 31. PLM OPK based at Łask was the first unit in the Polish air arm to suffer a Lim-2 loss. On 19 January 1955 1st Lt Witold J. Wallas, having completed an exercise in the manoeuvring area, lost spatial orientation in the clouds. The aircraft crashed in the village of Radzikowo Stare near Czerwińsk and Wisłą. The pilot was killed.

The second Lim-2 was lost in a crash on 18 May 1955 in the 26. PLM. 2nd Lt Marian Wolszczak lost spatial orientation in the clouds during an interception sortie in a two-ship formation. He ejected, but was killed. The aircraft crashed into Łebsko lake. On 25 September 1956 1st Lt Zygmunt Gościniak from the 26. PLM, based at Zegrze Pomorskie, fled to Bornholm in Lim-2 "1327" (s/n 1B-01327). During a practice aerial combat sortie in a two-ship formation with a Soviet pilot at an altitude of 6,000 m he took advantage of the situation when his aircraft was behind the Russian's aircraft and he was flying lower. He did not turn following the leader, but he turned

133

[133]: Lim-2 "921" (s/n 1B-00921) of the 1. PLM. Warsaw-Babice airfield, 1957.

[134]: Lim-2s "911" and "1030" of the 1. PLM. The "1030" (s/n 1B-01030) was lost in an accident while towing a target drogue on 24 July 1958. The pilot ejected.

in the opposite direction and dived to an altitude of 100 m. Despite the failure of his compass and lack of a map he made it to Rønne airfield. He made a belly landing on grass, damaging the starboard wing. On 4 February 1958 a crash of the Lim-2 "411", which took off from Zegrze Pomorskie air base for an interception sortie, occurred. Two minutes after take-off the aircraft flown by 1st Lt Jerzy Matuszewski lost radio contact. The pilot probably lost spatial orientation in the clouds. He died in the aircraft which crashed 14 km away from the airfield. Another tragic crash, in which two pilots were lost, took place in the 26. PLM on 21 March 1960. During a target drogue firing exercise over Pomianowo near Zegrze Pomorskie, a Lim-2 and Lim-5 aircraft collided in the air. There were no bailout attempts. Second Lieutenants Tadeusz Golon and Piotr Piotrów were killed. Less than two months later, on 12 May 1960 the 26. PLM lost another Lim-2 aircraft with a pilot in a crash. During a day flight with the use of the blind landing system in bad weather conditions, after the aircraft cleared out of the overcast radio contact was lost. The Lim-2 crashed near Niekłonice, 5 km away from Koszalin. The pilot, 2nd Lt Mieczysław Leloch, was killed. There was no bailout attempt and the cause of the crash was not found.

Another pilot's escape abroad in a Lim-2 aircraft took place in the 31. PLM on 7 November 1957. 1st Lt Bogdan Kożuchowski

[135]: After service in the 1. PLM the Lim-2 "921" was transferred to OSL-4 at Dęblin in January 1958. Note the shape of the digit "2", probably hand-painted by a mechanic.

took off from Łask air base in the Lim-2 "1919" (s/n 1B-01919). On his last drops of fuel he made it to the Swedish coast and landed wheels up in the Halland region, in the southern part of the country. As an aftermath of this escape the regiment was reformed as 31. Combat Training Regiment (31. PSz-B) in May 1958. It was detached from the 5. DLM OPK and became part of the structure of Radom-based OSL-5. All Lim-5 aircraft were transferred to other units. The 31. PSz-B operated Lim-2 aircraft until disbandment in 1963. On 4 June 1958 at the base of the 31. PLM at Łask a crash of a Lim-2, which was at the disposal of the commander of OSL-5, took place. The duty technician of the 2nd Squadron of the 31. PLM, 2nd Lt Stanisław Mróz, started the engine without authorization and took off. The aircraft climbed to about 20 m above ground level, crashed and burned. 2nd Lt Mróz was killed. The next crash took place in the 31. PSz-B on 1 March 1961. Due to unknown reasons "717" (s/n 1B-00714) crashed and exploded near the village of Żabiełów, a dozen or so kilometers away from Łask air base. The pilot, Capt. Wiesław Żuławiński, was killed. During a practice ground strafing sortie on 31 May 1962 the engine of Lim-2 "1620" (s/n 1B-01620) flamed out. The aircraft hit the airfield fence during the emergency landing and groundlooped. The pilot, 2nd Lt Marian Brzeziński, survived and the aircraft was scrapped.

The 39. PLM, based at Mierzęcice began to re-equip with Lim-2 aircraft, more advanced than the Lim-1, in early June 1955. On the night of 23 August 1955 a crash of Lim-2 "617" (s/n 1B-00617) took place. 2nd Lt Ryszard Szmit lost spatial orientation after an attack on a towed target. The aircraft crashed near the village of Wierzby, district Lubliniec. The pilot was killed. In September 1955 the 39. PLM flew the first bombing sorties in the Lim-2 aircraft on targets on the Błędowska Desert range

[136]: Lim-2 "1012" of Capt. Ryszard Grundman, with a later version of the red lightning bolt.

[137]: Lim-2 "1106" of the 34. PLM MW in flight over Pomerania.

from an altitude of 3,500 m and 60-degree angle. In mid-June 1956 the first night training sorties in bad weather conditions were flown. Numerous high altitude flights were flown. 1st Lt Jerzy Brzosko attained the highest altitude of 14,200 m in a Lim-2.

The 39. PLM received aircraft of, among others, the 19th production batch: "1915", "1917", "1920", "1921", "1922" and "1930". On 13 September 1956 one of the regiment's squadrons with the Lim-2 aircraft was moved from Mierzęcice to Powidz, to the 38. PLM being formed there. Aircraft number "1931", operated previously by OSL-4 at Dęblin, was also transferred to Powidz. During practice before an air parade in September 1959 Lim-2 "1905" was lost. The pilot bailed out after the engine failed. During an airshow on Rybnik airfield on 25 September 1960 a Lim-2 of the 39. PLM went into a spin and crashed during an aerobatics display. The pilot, Capt. Kazimierz Gielas, was killed.

In 1956 the first lot of Lim-2 aircraft was delivered to the 11. PLM, based at Debrzno. Older Lim-1 aircraft were gradually transferred to attack units. The first Lim-2, "620" (s/n 1B-00620), was lost in a crash on 16 August 1957 during a flight of Debrzno-based aircraft to Mińsk Mazowiecki. A two-ship formation, in which 2nd Lt Józef Grób was flying, was turned back to Debrzno. On approach to landing his Lim-2 "620" went into spin from a height of 50 m due to pilot error and crashed near the runway. The second Lim-2 crash in the 11. PLM took place on 24 April 1959. 2nd Lt Zygmunt Portko was doing aerobatics at low altitude. His Lim-2 "1821" (s/n 1B-01821) stalled and went into a spin. The pilot jettisoned the canopy but did not eject. He died in the aircraft, which crashed near the village of Ogorzeliny, district Człuchów. On 17 July 1960, during the parade on the anniversary of the battle of Grunwald (the first battle of Tannenberg), 16 Lim-2

138

[138]: Lim-2s "1111" and "1422" of Babimost-based 45. PLM, second half of the 1950s. The Lim-2 "1111" (s/n 1B-01111) was lost in a crash in the 61. PSz-B based at Nowe Miasto n. Pilicą in 1962.

139

[139]: Lim-2 "1117" (s/n 1B011-17) of the 34. PLM MW. In this aircraft LtJG Leon Karkut won the title of "Ace" in 1956 and the aircraft was marked with the red lightning bolt of an "outstanding crew".

and Lim-5 aircraft from the 11. PLM formed the left box in the "plate" formation. The third Lim-2 crash in the 11. PLM occurred on 20 November 1964. 1st Lt Tadeusz Gawrysiak was killed when flying through clouds on approach to landing at Debrzno air base in bad weather. He crashed in the village of Niwy, 7.5 km away from the base. The Lim-2, "713" (s/n 1B-00713), was lost.[1]

On 16 April 1965 the 11. PLM lost Lim-2 "1727" (s/n 1B-01727), piloted by Capt. Eugeniusz Maćkowski, during a night flight in bad weather. On approach to landing the aircraft flew into trees at a height of 5–6 m, but the pilot managed to climb and bail out from an altitude of 600–700 m. The aircraft crashed several kilometers away from Debrzno air base. In the fourth Lim-2 crash in the 11. PLM, on 13 June 1967 2nd Lt Józef Szymański was killed. The Lim-2 "1117" (s/n 1B-01117) with the pilot in the cockpit crashed due to unknown s in the village of Bożydar near Kórnik. The 11. PLM lost Lim-2 "927" due to a pilot error. On 26 August 1967 Capt. Zygmunt Morakowski, landing at an unfamiliar airfield at Pruszcz Gdański, did not lower the landing gear, which the duty ground controller failed to notice. The aircraft skidded 700 m on the runway, caught fire and burned. The pilot managed to escape from the burning aircraft. On 30 September 1967 the 11. PLM assumed the number and tradition of wartime 9. PLM, formed in the USSR in 1944. Then in 1968 the 9. PLM was transferred from the Air Defence to the Air Force. In 1972 a blown tyre of the taxiing Lim-2 "1626" led to the collision with a MiG-21M. The damaged MiG-21M was repaired, while the Lim-2 (s/n 1B-01626) was used in 1973 for conversion of an SBLim-1 two-seater (s/n 1A- 08003), to an SBLim-2. Thanks to deliveries of new aircraft from WSK Mielec and rotation of aircraft from other units during 1955–1973, about 80 Lim-2 aircraft went through the inventory of the Debrzno-based 11. PLM. These were, among others, aircraft from the 4th and 5th production batches, with tactical numbers "201", "205", "215", "318", "401", "404", "407", "409", "417", "418", "419", "502", "513", "516", "517", "526", "529" and from later batches "713", "827", "909", "926", "927", "1001", "1013", "1117", "1118", "1315", "1319", "1413", "1517", "1603", "1619", "1621", "1705" and "1727".

In the autumn of 1955 the first Lim-2 fighters were delivered to the 3. PLM, based at Wrocław-Strachowice airfield. This regiment, a part of the 6. DLM, had previously operated S-102 and Lim-1 fighters. On 24 January 1956 a Lim-2 crash occurred. Probably the underwing tank was ripped out during the turn to finals The pilot lost control of the aircraft, which crashed near the village of Owczary, district Oława. 1st Lt Ryszard Krasowski was killed. The second Lim-2 crash in the 3. PLM took place on 5 May 1956. 2nd Lt Stanisław W. Karczewski was killed during a training sortie near Wrocław. On 21 July 1961 the Lim-2 "514" (s/n 1B-00514), flown by 2nd Lt Tadeusz Styczyński, was lost due to pilot error. On approach to landing by day in bad weather the aircraft hit the ground control van and then the antenna van with the landing gear and then hit the ground with the wing and fuselage. The aircraft was scrapped and the pilot sustained minor injuries. Another Lim-2 was lost in the 3. PLM on 26 June 1964 at Wrocław airfield. During the flying day the landing direction was changed due to the change of the wind direction, but the mobile ground control station was

1 Records of the aircraft crashes during 1961–1980 are mostly based on publications by Sławomir Bartosik, Robert Senkowski and Miłosz Bogdański "Crashed, failures and damaged in the Polish air arm 1961–1970 and 1971–1980".

[140]: Lim-2s "1119", "1017", "1107" and "1311" of the 39. PLM at Mierzęcice air base in 1957.

140

[141]: Lim-2s "1213", "1619" and "0716" of Piła-based 51. PLMSz, armed with FAB 100 bombs before a sortie to Wędrzyn bombing range.

not relocated and radio communication was not established. The observer in the ground control station saw Lim-2 "1718" on approach with the landing gear up and fired five warning flares. 2nd Lt Kazimierz Michałowski failed to notice the flares and touched down on the runway with the wheels up. The aircraft caught fire and burned, but the pilot managed to escape. In 1967 the regiment regained the original number "11" and traditions of the 11. PLM, which flew the first combat mission from Białęgi airfield on 24 April 1945.

The first Lim-2 fighters were delivered to the 34. PLM MW in mid-1954. In early 1955 the regiment had 18 Lim-1 and 12 new Lim-2 aircraft. In February further Lim-2 aircraft arrived. Due to bad weather conditions, some aircraft received from WSK Mielec factory were not test flown at an altitude of 15,000 m, thus were not cleared for flying at that altitude. In the 34. PLM Lt. Cdr Romuald Rozmysłowicz and Lt Lesław Węgrzynowski were cleared for these test flights and performed them on newly delivered aircraft. On 1 October 1955 the regiment's combat inventory included 24 Lim-2 and 19 Lim-1 aircraft. During night flights in fair weather a crash of Lim-2 "1109" (s/n 1B-01109) took place. LTJG Józef Madejewski lost spatial orientation and crashed into the sea about 600–700 m north of Karwia. On 31 January 1957 in the inventory of the 34. PLM were 24 Lim-2 aircraft with tactical numbers "107", "111", "112", "502", "508", "510", "512", "601", "1007", "1016", "1020", "1103", "1105", "1106", "1110", "1112", "1113", "1115", "1116", "1117", "1118", "1121", "1122" and "1129". During an exercise on a sea gunnery range near Babie Doły a crash took place. Ensign Jerzy Bielichowski, flying Lim-2 "1020" (s/n 1B-01020), lost spatial orientation and crashed into the sea 3 km north of Oksywie torpedo test facility. The pilot was killed. In 1958 the regiment also operated the Lim-2 aircraft with tactical numbers "106", "115", "915", "917", "1203", "1205", "1216", "1312" "1322", "1409". During advanced flying training in a three-ship formation two aircraft collided in the air. The Lim-2 "1409" (s/n 1B-01409), flown by LTJG Tomasz Ziaja, lost the left part of the vertical stabilizer. The Lim-2 "1312" (s/n 1B-01312) of LTJG Marian Klusek sustained heavier damage of the skin, frames and fuselage upper spar belt between the frames. The pilots landed at their home base and the aircraft were sent for overhaul by the Field Aircraft Repair Works. In January 1959 the first 12 Lim-5 aircraft, with better flying and tactical capability, entered the inventory of the 34. PLM. During the next year the Lim-2s began to be withdrawn and on 20 October there were 16 of them in the regiment's inventory. On 13 June 1961 Lt Henryk Wojtecki lost spatial orientation while flying Lim-2 "1007" (s/n 1B-01007) and crashed into the Bay of Gdańsk. In 1963 two pilots were killed in crashes and two aircraft were lost due to failures. On 19 March 1963 at Babie Doły airfield the Lim-2 "1105" rolled off of the runway due to pilot error and hit a concrete wall. The aircraft was scrapped. Three months later, on 25 June, after an interception and practice air-to-air engagement, a Lim-5 hit the fuselage and wing of the Lim-2 "1322" (s/n 1B-01322), piloted by Ens. Ireneusz Tygielski, who died in his aircraft near Brodnica Górna. The Lim-5 pilot ejected. The third Lim-2 crash in 1963 took place in the 34. PLM on 15 October. The negligence of the ground crews caused the crash of the Lim-2 "1112" (s/n 1B-01112) and death of LtJG Janusz Grzelak. Fumes of kerosene penetrating into the cockpit just after take-off made flying impossible. The pilot lost spatial orientation and died in the aircraft, which hit the ground. In 1966 sixteen Lim-2 were withdrawn from the regiment. In the autumn of that year there were no aircraft of this type in the unit's inventory.

The 29. PLM, based at Orneta operated MiG-15 aircraft in 1953. Later it was equipped with the Lim-1 and subsequently the Lim-2. In the first lot serial numbers: 1B-02007, 1B-02012, 1B-02015, 1B-02017, 1B-02019, 1B-03001, 1B-03005, 1B-03010, 1B-06002, 1B-07007, 1B-07020, 1B-08014, 1B-08026, 1B-08027

[142]: Lim-2 "1216" (s/n 1B012-16) among the aircraft of the 34. PLM MW at Goleniów airfield before the air parade over Szczecin on the occasion of the Navy Day in June 1958.

and 1B-09029 were delivered. As result of aircraft rotation, the Orneta-based regiment operated several dozen Lim-2s from various production batches, including the 19th. On 12 April 1956 a Lim-2 crash took place. 1st Lt Jan Krześniak, flying with the use of the blind landing system by day in bad weather, lost spatial orientation in clouds. He was killed in the aircraft, which crashed at Kolonia Babiak, 14 km away from Orneta air base. Half a year later, on 22 October another Lim-2 crash in the 29. PLM took place. On approach to landing at night in bad weather, with the use of the blind landing system, 1st Lt Eugeniusz Czarnecki lost spatial orientation in the clouds. He was killed in the aircraft that crashed in the village of Mingajny, 8 km away from the air base. On 12 June 1962 a Lim-2 was lost due to failure caused by pilot error. During aerial combat training 2nd Lt Andrzej Wanowicz stalled the aircraft, which went into a spin. The pilot ejected and the aircraft fell into Mildzkie lake, 14 km away from Orneta. In the mid-1960s the combat lineup of the 29. PLM comprised three squadrons. The 1st Pursuit Squadron was equipped with Lim-5 aircraft, while the 2nd Fighter Squadron operated 12 Lim-2 fighters. The 3rd Squadron was also equipped with Lim-2s. When landing at Orneta air base on 23 September 1966 the pilot of Lim-2 "1029" (s/n 1B-01029) could not lower the landing gear. Either the left or right strut could be lowered. The Lim-2 "1029" was damaged on landing on two wheels. It was not repaired and was written off in 1967. Another Lim-2 was lost due to a failure on 16 February 1968. 1st Lt Wacław Matejek made an error on take-off from Orneta air base. Lim-2 "616" (s/n 1B-00616), climbing prematurely at a speed of 220–230 km/h and critical angle of attack, crashed and caught fire. The pilot was rescued from the wreckage. On 5 June 1968, during a flying exercise 2nd Lt Edward Urban was killed in Lim-2 "704" (s/n 1B-00704). Radio contact with him was lost when he commenced medium flying practice over the sea. The cause of the crash was not determined, as neither the pilot, nor the wreckage were found. Only the floating dinghy, oxygen mask and flight helmet were found in the sea. The 29. PLM was disbanded on 1 February 1969.

During the service of Lim-2 fighters in the 28. PLM, based at Redzikowo air base near Słupsk, six aircraft were lost in five crashes and one failure. The first Lim-2 crash in the 28. PLM took place on the night of 14 July 1956. 2nd Lt Marian Gruszka took off for a night sortie in fair weather. During the second turn his Lim-2 crashed in the village of Wielogłowy near Redzikowo, killing the pilot. The crash was probably caused by the failure of the aileron control system. On 5 July 1957 1st Lt Henryk Bednarek, a pilot of the 28. PLM undergoing training in the 2. PLM at Cracow-Rakowice airfield, went into a spin due to his error during a medium flying training sortie. The Lim-2 crashed in inverted flight near the village of Kończyce, killing the pilot. During a training sortie on 2 April 1958 two Lim-2s of the 28. PLM collided in the air. Both pilot ejected. 2nd Lt Zygmunt Kostrzewski landed safely by parachute, while 2nd Lt Henryk Łoskot was killed near the village of Szpon, because his parachute failed to open. On 25 February 1961 2nd Lt Jan Rozbicki exhausted the entire fuel supply during medium flying training in Lim-2 "1402" (s/n 1B-01402) and the engine stopped. Instead of bailing out, the pilot attempted to land with flaps up in hilly terrain. He was killed in the destroyed aircraft near the village of Żoruchowo, 14 km away from Słupsk. The last Lim-2 crash in the 28. PLM took place on 2 December 1964. On approach to landing 2nd Lt Ryszard Dąbrowski made a flying error when descending through the cloud layer. He was killed in "714" (s/n 1B-00714), which made an increasingly steep turn and crashed in the village of Potęgowo, 20 km away from the airfield.

Lim-2 aircraft were delivered to the 38. PLM based at Powidz along with the squadron detached from Mierzęcice-based 39. PLM. On 14 December 1956 in the combat inventory of the Powidz-based regiment were 17 Lim-2 aircraft: "203" (s/n 1B-00203), "410" (s/n 1B-00410), "504" (s/n 1B-00504), "513" (s/n 1B 00513), "520" (s/n 1B-00520), "608" (s/n 1B-00608), "609" (s/n 1B-00609), "613" (s/n 1B-00613), "704" (s/n 1B-00704), "813" (s/n 1B-00813), "814" (s/n 1B-00814), "905" (s/n 1B-00905), "907" (s/n 1B-00907), "909" (s/n 1B-00909), "1223" (s/n 1B-01223), "1229" (s/n 1B-01229) and "1302" (s/n 1B-01302). The inventory was supplemented by eight previously operated MiG-15bis aircraft. In April 1957 sixteen Lim-2 fighters were prepared for summer operations, beside 10 MiG-15bis fighters still in service. In July 1957 the regiment received eight Lim-2s from Dęblin: "618" and seven examples of the last production batch, with numbers "1925" through "1931", on which foreign pilots were trained in the "Group 100". A column of 25 aircraft from the 38. PLM, consisting of 19 Lim-2s, tactical numbers: "520", "615", "813", "905", "909", "1005", "1006", "1011", "1215", "1223", "1302", "1814", "1909", "1926", "1927", "1928", "1929", "1930" and "1931", and 6 MiG-15bis, was a part of the "herringbone" formation, displayed on 8 September 1957 during the Aviation Day air show at Warsaw Bemowo/Babice airfield. On the night of 18 September 1957 2nd Lt Bolesław Majewski, flying in Lim-2 "1302" (s/n 1B-01302), did not return from a two-ship sortie. His aircraft crashed in the village of Otorowo near Solec Kujawski. The cause of the crash was not found. The pilot ejected, but was killed because his prematurely deployed parachute wrapped around him during

143

[143]: Lim-2 "1216" of the 58. PSz-B in the lead position of the "1000" parade formation, consisting of Lim-2 aircraft. The aircraft has the tips of the underwing tanks painted red with a black outline. Dęblin air base, 1966.

[144]: The "1000" formation, consisting of 43 Lim-2 aircraft, demonstrated over Plac Defilad (Parade Square) in Warsaw on 22 July 1966.

144

145

[145]: Lim-2s "1223" and "1225" of the 13. PLM before the air parade over Warsaw on 22 July 1956. The Lim-2 "1223" (s/n 1B-01223) was assigned to Powidz-based 38. PLM in 1956 and was operated there until the unit's disbandment in 1958. In 1962 it was written off after an emergency landing with engine off when operated by the 45. PLM, based at Babimost.

146

[146]: The Lim-2 "1301" (s/n 1B-01301) was one of 24 aircraft transferred from the Air Defence to the Air Force during change of dependence of Debrzno-based 11. PLM.

[147]: Lim-2 "1302" (s/n 1B-01302) of the 38. PLM based at Powidz. This aircraft was lost in a crash on 18 September 1957.

147

148

[148]: Lim-2 "608" (s/n 1B-00608) of the 39. PLM based at Mierzęcice. It was transferred to the 38. PLM based at Powidz and was operated by this regiment during 1956–1958.

the ejection. On 2 January 1958 in the combat inventory of the 38. PLM were 24 Lim-2 aircraft (tactical numbers: "203", "513", "520", "608", "613", "618", "704", "813", "905", "907", "909", "1005"?, "1006", "1009", "1011", "1223", "1229", "1814", "1925", "1926", "1927", "1928", "1929" and "1930") and 12 MiG-15bis still in service. The 38. PLM was disbanded on 1 August 1958 and on its basis Advanced Pilot Training School at Modlin began to be formed.

The 40. PLM, based at Świdwin was a part of the 11. PLM. On 10 April 1956 the regiment received ten new Lim-2 aircraft from the WSK Mielec factory. The Lim-2 pilots of the 40. PLM took part in the greatest air parade of Polish aviation during the Aviation Day air show at Warsaw Bemowo/Babice on 8 September 1957. The parade and air show was conducted among others by 333 Lim-2s from various units. The flypast of four 75-ship Lim-2 formations was demonstrated. During the flypast the Lim-2s of the 40. PLM flew over the spectators in the fourth 75-ship column. During the exercise in September 1957 sorties were flown from Świdwin and Goleniów airfields. The Lim-2s of the 40. PLM participating in that exercise escorted a bomber squadron, making a mock nuclear bombing attack on the Drawsko Pomorskie range. In January 1958 the Świdwin-based regiment had 29 Lim-2 fighters in its inventory. On 4 February 1958 2nd Lt Henryk Wieczorek was killed in

149 *[149]: Lim-2 "716" (s/n 1B 00716) of the 62. PLM, based at Krzesiny.*

a crash. Flying a Lim-2 he lost spatial orientation in the clouds and hit the ground. The next Lim-2 crash in the 40. PLM took place on 13 August 1959 during a day formation flight in good weather. 2nd Lt Jerzy Rybakowicz was killed. His aircraft crashed near the village of Biały Zdrój.

In December 1956 the 19. LEH received the first two Lim-2 aircraft – "1515" (s/n 1B-01515) and "1520" (s/n 1B-01520). They were used for sorties over Mrzeżyno gunnery range. From May 1958 the 19. LEH was based at Słupsk-Redzikowo airfield. In the same year the unit received a third Lim-2, "908" (s/n 1B-00908). The squadron received the next three Lim-2s in 1965. These were: "119" (s/n 1B-00119) (from the oldest, 1st production batch), "605" (s/n 1B-00605) and "1229" (s/n 1B-01229). The last Lim-2s ("301" and "1229") remained in the inventory of the 19. LEH until 1971.

In the Goleniów-based 4. PLM, assigned to the 11. DLM, two Lim-2 crashes took place. The first tragedy occurred on 7 May 1958 during a two-ship low-level flight. The Lim-2 flown by 2nd Lt Waldemar Boniewski hit a tree and then a residential building in the village of Brzozowo. The building burned with a family of four inside and the pilot was killed. In the second Lim-2 crash in the 4. PLM, on 17 July 1959 1st Lt Eugeniusz Chmielewski was killed. The 4. PLM based at Goleniów was renamed to 4. PLM "Cracow " in May 1967.

The 62. PSz-T LM based at Krzesiny received the first Lim-2 aircraft in 1955. In 1957 the regiment was renamed 62. PLM. During an aerial combat practice over the village of Wiry near Krzesiny on 26 June 1958 a Lim-2 collided in the air with a Lim-5. The Lim-5 pilot, 2nd Lt Jerzy Tokarski, was killed, while the Lim-2 pilot safely ejected. A double fatal crash took place in the 62. PLM on 25 August 1959, during a two-ship formation flight. Two Lim-2 fighters collided in the air and crashed near the village of Leśniczówka. 1st Lt Zbigniew Adamek and 2nd Lt Jan Kulka were killed.

The 51. PLSz, based at Piła air base from 1954, was equipped with Il-10 attack aircraft. Only in 1957 did it begin to re-equip with Lim-1 aircraft, withdrawn from fighter units. Then Lim-2 aircraft also arrived. On 6 October 1959 a Lim-2 crash took place. 1st Lt Józef Witkiewicz was killed during an emergency landing at Toruń airfield. In 1960 the regiment was renamed to fighter-attack (51. PLM-Sz). On 24 May 1962 a Lim-2 crash in the 51 PLM-Sz took place during a practice low-level basic flying sortie. 2nd Lt Paweł Wrzesień went below the minimum altitude. His Lim-2 "1522" hit trees in a steep turn in the village of Próchnowo and crashed. A year later, on 21 May 1963 in another crash over the Piła air base during medium flying practice 2nd Lt Tadeusz Statuch was killed. Due to pilot error the Lim-2 "408" stalled, went into spin and crashed near the airfield.

The 5. PLSz also converted from the Il-10 to Lim-1 and Lim-2 aircraft. Conversion to jet aircraft was completed as late as 1960. After the conversion, in July 1960 the regiment was renamed to fighter-attack. In January 1960 two Lim-2 crashes took place in the 5. PLSz. In the first of them, on 15 January 1960 Capt. Marek Orłowski was killed when passing through the clouds with the use of the blind landing system. His aircraft crashed near the village of Czarnowo, district Toruń. Another one occurred only ten days later. During a practice night sortie in bad weather a Lim-2 crashed due to an unknown reason 12 km away from Bydgoszcz- Szwederowo airfield. The pilot, 2nd Lt Jan Tatarewicz, was killed. On 16 January 1961, during an unfortunate night landing in bad weather with the use of the blind landing system, Lim-2 "101" (s/n 1B-00101) was lost. The aircraft was scrapped and the pilot, 2nd Lt Jerzy Paluszkiewicz, was unhurt. In the "herringbone" formation, consisting of four nine-ship Vic flights, displayed during an air parade over Warsaw on 22 July 1964 the third vic was formed of Lim-2s from the 5. PLM-Sz. In 1965 the unit was renamed 5. PLM-B (*Pułk Lotnictwa Myśliwsko-Bombowego* – Fighter-Bomber Aviation Regiment). In 1967 the regiment regained its original number 3 and name "*Pomorski*" (Pomeranian). On 6 August 1968 a double Lim-2 crash took place in the 3. PLM-B. The Lim-2s "206" and "619" crashed near Osowa Góra, 8 km away from the airfield. The pilots, 2nd Lt Lech Zarębski and 1st Lt Piotr Barawąs, were killed.

[150]: Lim-2 "1322" (s/n 1B-01322) of the 34. PLM MW. It was lost in a crash on 25 June 1963. The Lim-2 "1409" (sixth in the line) was delivered factory-fresh to the 25. PLM based at Pruszcz Gdański. When operated by the 34. PLM MW it collided in the air with the Lim-2 "1312", after which both aircraft landed safely. After the repair the Lim-2 "1409" still flew in the 34. PLM and during 25–30 November 1965 it was transferred to the 26. PLM, based at Zegrze Pomorskie. This photo was taken at Goleniów airfield in June 1959.

150

[151]: Lim-2 "1409" (s/n 1B-01409) ended its service on a railway platform, used in the Polish Railways for removing snow and ice from rails and junctions with the hot exhaust gases.

The 53. PLSz based at Mirosławiec, equipped with the Il-10 aircraft, began reorganization and conversion to Lim-2 jet aircraft in 1959. The aircrews were trained in the Independent Operational Aviation Conversion Centre at Bydgoszcz. As early as 8 August 1959 the commander of the 53. PLSz, Lt Col. Tadeusz Gientkowski soloed in a Lim-2. In 1960, after the introduction of the Lim-2s, the unit was renamed to 53. PLM-Sz. In late 1960 in the regiment's inventory were 18 Lim-2 aircraft and in the next year the number increased to 24. Problems with operation of the weary Lim-2s arose. During intense training tragic events were unavoidable. Due to bad organization of the flying pattern on 20 July 1962 the Lim-2 "930", flown by 2nd Lt Zbigniew Frankowski, collided on approach to landing with Lim-2 "113", flown by 2nd Lt Bogdan Dusza. The "930" went into steep dive and crashed, killing the pilot. Despite the clipped wingtip and limited controllability 2nd Lt Dusza managed to climb to an altittude of 300 m and ejected between Łowicz Wałecki and Kalisz Pomorski. In late 1962 a considerable number of jet aircraft had to be sent for overhaul due to little flying time left on the airframes. Only 19 Lim-2 and Lim-2R single seaters and eight two seat combat trainers remained in service. On 19 March 1963, during a low-level flight over Kalisz Pomorski railway station, Lim-2R "1416" hit treetops a few kilometers away from the station. 2nd Lt Jan Borer landed safely in the damaged aircraft, which was repaired and returned to service. Several months later, in August, the same aircraft hit the fence of the Mirosławiec air base due to malfunctioning brakes. The aircraft was repaired in No. 4 Military Aircraft Repair Works. In the "herringbone" formation, consisting of four nine-ship Vic flights, displayed during an air parade over Warsaw on 22 July 1964, the fourth Vic was formed of Lim-2s from the 53. PLM-Sz.

Equipping the fighter-attack regiments with Lim-1 and then Lim-2 aircraft was an interim solution, as they lacked rocket

[152]: Lim-2 "1323" (s/n 1B-01323) of the 39. PLM, Mierzęcice, 1957.

armament, necessary for attacking ground targets efficiently. They had not enough fuel tank and external weapon stations. This branch of aviation was to be eventually equipped with Lim-5M and Lim-6 fighter attack aircraft.

On 6 February 1960, a fatal Lim-2 crash took place during a technical test flight after an engine change. Capt. Sławomir Ziółkowski, a test pilot in the Air Force Institute of Technology, was performing a medium flying exercise over Warsaw Bemowo/Babice airfield. Upon completion of the exercise he flew over the airfield in inverted position, descending uncontrollably. Returning to upright and level flight he crashed on Duchnicka street in Warsaw.

The 41. PLM, based at Malbork, received Lim-1 aircraft in 1954 and later Lim-2s. On 17 November 1960, during a day aerial combat exercise in good weather, 2nd Lt Henryk Tyliński was killed. On 18 May 1961 four Lim-2 aircraft took off from Malbork air base for a medium flying practice in diamond formation. During recovery from a loop in formation near the airfield, Lim-2 "1622" began to overtake Lim-2 "1614", hitting the leading edge of its wing and damaging it along with the pitot probe. Both aircraft landed safely, were repaired and returned to service. (The Lim-2 "1614" was converted to the Lim-2R reconnaissance variant and operated by the 21. PLR-T (*Pułk Lotnictwa Rozpoznania Taktycznego* – Tactical Reconnaissance Aviation Regiment). Two crashes took place in the 41. PLM in 1964. On 19 February 1st Lt Stanisław Kublik was killed in Lim-2 "1515", probably due to faintness. Eight days later, on 27 February, Lim-2 "1206" crashed due to pilot error during approach to landing at night in bad weather with the use of the blind landing system. The pilot, 1st Lt Marcjan Pierścionek, was killed. During a day medium flying training sortie in fair weather Lim-2 "1926" crashed. In the final phase of recovery from a stall turn the aircraft crashed in the village of Postolin, 23 km away from Malbork airfield. The pilot, 2nd Lt Jan Borys, was killed. The last Lim-2 was lost in the 41. PLM on 21 October 1971, due to an engine failure during a night flight in bad weather. After take-off from Malbork and interception of the target the task called for landing at Debrzno air base. The engine quit at an altitude of 50–70 meters. The Lim-2 "814" touched down with landing gear lowered in the forest 800 meters short of the runway. The pilot, Capt. Tadeusz Barański, survived and the aircraft was scrapped.

The 45. PLM was formed in 1957 at Babimost airfield on the basis of the 3rd Squadron of the 1. PLM. Initially it was equipped with MiG-15 aircraft. They were replaced by Polish-built Lim-1s and Lim-2s. On 4 May 1961 a crash of Lim-2 "1903" occurred. During a night flight in fair weather a corroded hydraulic reservoir broke. The aircraft crashed on the village of Nowe Kramsko near Babimost. 1st Lt Jerzy Sajewski had no time to bail out. Due to fuel pump failure 1st Lt Czesław Reut landed in Lim-2 with no power off-airport near Kamień Pomorski airfield. The aircraft was written off. On 9 May 1967 during a night flight in good weather 2nd Lt Ludwik Blacha descended too low and Lim-2 "1906" hit trees in a forest and crashed in a field 1 km away from Sulechów. The pilot was killed. The Lim-2 "809" and Lim-5P "607", returning from night sorties, collided during landing. The Lim-5P was repaired, while Lim-2 (s/n 1B-00809) was scrapped. The aft fuselage was used for a conversion to an SBLim-2 two-seater. The forward fuselage section was taken from a Czechoslovak CS-102 (s/n 612782) "682" (?).

The 2. PLM, based at Cracow Rakowice-Czyżyny, was a part of the 7. DLM. It operated first the Yak-23 and then MiG-15 fighters. In August 1954 the regiment handed over its last Yak-23s to OSL-5 and received Lim-1 and later Lim-2 aircraft. On 14 October 1958 1st Lt Jerzy Bigaj was killed on landing in a Lim-2 at Cracow-Balice airfield, due to a throttle lever jam. Another Lim-2 crash in the 2. PLM took place on 12 September 1962. 1st Lt Stefan Mierzejewski took off for an advanced flying training sortie. Lim-2 "1101" went into a spin and the pilot was not able to eject. The aircraft crashed 5 km away from Balice airfield. In 1963 the regiment was moved to Łask. On 6 January 1964 Lim-2 "821" was lost due to a failure during a low-level interception sortie. The aircraft caught fire due to a fuel leak from the high-pressure fuel system. 1st Lt Tadeusz Kłósak ejected from the burning aircraft, but suffered a spinal injury. In 1967 the regiment regained its number "10", returning to the traditions of the combat-proven unit. On 5 April 1968, during night flights of the 3rd Squadron of the 10. PLM Lim-2 "1902" crashed, when 2nd Lt Cezary Owczarek was returning from a training sortie. The aircraft,

[153]: Lim-2 "1430" (s/n 1B-01430) was delivered factory-fresh to the 25. PLM based at Pruszcz Gdańsk in January 1956. On 22 November 1962 it was still in the regiment's inventory.

153

[154]: Lim-2s "1516" and "1520" of the 19. LEH. Standing behind them in line are Lim-2s of the 40. PLM. The two airmen are 1st Lt Grzywnowicz and 1st Lt Firganek – navigators of the 19. LEH. Świdwin air base, 1957.

155

[155]: Lim-2 aircraft participating in the airshow on 8 September 1957 on the runway of Babice airfield in Warsaw. Lim-2s "1910", "1629" and "1619" are from Orneta-based 29. PLM, "1315", "1316" and "1319" are from Krzesiny-based 62. PLM, "1401" and "1102" are from 2. PLM "Cracow," 1309", "1012", "927", "1001" and "1026" are from 1. PLM "Warsaw".

with landing gear lowered, crashed 900 meters short of the runway threshold. The pilot was killed.

The 30. PLSz MW received its first Lim-2 aircraft in August 1957. On 1 December 1960 there were 20 Lim-2 and 12 Lim-1 aircraft in the regiment's inventory. The 30. PLSz MW was based at Siemirowice, (along with the 15. SELR MW – Naval Independent Reconnaissance Aviation Squadron). Three years later the regiment was renamed fighter-attack. On 5 December 1963, due to errors made on landing, Lim-2 "601" was lost. 2nd Lt Zdzisław Maciński hit the ground with the nosewheel first on touchdown, causing the aircraft to bounce several meters high multiple times and break the nosewheel strut. The aircraft hit the runway, which ruptured the main fuel tank and caused a fire. The pilot managed to escape from the burning aircraft. The night practice bombing sortie in good weather against an illuminated surface target on the Bay of Puck bombing range on 19 September 1966 ended with a tragedy. Lim-2 "510" crashed into the sea on the traverse of Hel, killing the pilot, 2nd Lt Kazimierz Staniewicz. In 1967 the regiment was renamed 7. PLM-Sz MW (*Pułk Lotnictwa Myśliwsko Szturmowego Marynarki Wojennej* – Naval Fighter-Attack Aviation Regiment). On 17 October 1968, during a night practice ground target bombing sortie in good weather on Strzepcz bombing range a crash of Lim-2 "1801" occurred. Instead of recovery from a dive after the bomb release, 2nd Lt Hieronim Katarzyński made a descending turn and crashed in the village of Osiek near the bombing range. The last Lim-2 aircraft were retired from the Naval Aviation on 15 June 1982.

In the latter half of the 1960s withdrawal of the Lim-2s from the fighter regiments and re-equipping with the MiG-21 and Lim-5 began. They were withdrawn from line units and transferred to combat training regiments. In 1958 the Lim-2s joined other types operated by the 59. PSz-B: a single MiG-15, two MiG-15bis and a dozen or so Lim-1s. They entered service quickly. In 1959 a team from this regiment, Capt. Jerzy Kozarek – leader, 1st Lt Henryk Marcinkiewicz – left wing, Capt. Czesław Kowalski – right wing and Capt. Feliks Pawlak – slot, demonstrated aerobatics at low and medium altitude (200–2,000 m) in a four-ship Lim-2 formation.

On 1 December 1959 in the inventory of the 59. PSz-B were 13 Lim-2 aircraft: "203", "218", "401", "413", "419", "513", "604", "815", "901", "913", "1008", "1627", "1703" and "1814". On 1 February 1962 1st Lt Henryk Marcinkiewicz was killed in a crash after having lost spatial orientation in clouds during a night flight. His Lim-2 "1601" crashed 14 km away from the airfield. On 6 July 1962 during a practice ground target strafing sortie an engine failure in Lim-2 "1125" occurred at an altitude of 700 m. The turbine RPM decreased rapidly, but the pilot, PFC Officer Cadet Henryk Janusz, turned toward the airfield. On landing the aircraft hit the radio van and crashed. The pilot survived with minor injuries. The aircrews of the 59. PSz-B demonstrated their flying skills on 22 July 1964 in an air parade over Warsaw. The "Roman Twenty" consisted of 26 Lim-2 aircraft. The second "herringbone" formation (four 9-ship vics) consisted of 36 Lim-2s. One of the four vics was composed of the Lim-2 aircraft from Biała Podlaska. In the autumn of 1964 the 59. PSz-B was disbanded and the aircraft were transferred to the 58. PSz-B at Dęblin and 61. PSz-B at Nowe Miasto nad Pilicą.

In Dęblin-based 58. PSz-B the Lim-2 aircraft remained in service until the 1980s. This regiment lost three aircraft of this type in crashes and four were scrapped after failures. Sgt Officer Cadet Jan Ragin was killed in a crash on 26 August 1964. An explosion on board occurred at an altitude of 800 m and the Lim-2 "309" began to lose height. The pilot jettisoned the canopy to bail out, but the ejection seat failed. Only after hitting the ground was the seat ejected with the pilot's body. The destroyed Lim-2 " 309" (s/n 1B-00309) had been operated in the Dęblin-based regiment since 1958. The cause of the crash was not found. Two years later, on 25 August 1966, the another Lim-2 crash took place and its cause was also not found. Lim-2 "905", flown by Sgt Officer Cadet Zbigniew Martewicz, hit the ground in the 6th minute of flight. On 12 August 1968, before

[156]: Lim-2s "1707" "1630" at Poznań-Krzesiny air base, home of the 62. PLM.

156

[157]: Lim-2 "1809" with expended cartridge case container after retirement from Siemirowice-based 7. PLM-Sz MW in 1982, photographed by Wacław Hołyś at Babimost air base, where it was ferried before being transferred to the Military Museum in Drzonów.

an airshow at Biała Podlaska airfield, a four-ship Lim-2 flight ("1309", "1311", "1815" and "1216") took off for a training sortie. Four pilots were to practice aerobatics over the airfield. The "1309", flown by Capt. Józef Kolmus, crashed in inverted flight. The pilot had no experience in such type of flying and died in the destroyed aircraft. In June 1969 the Lim-2 "1827" was lost. After an increase of engine RPM during a ground test vibrations occurred. The pilot managed to leave the aircraft, from which fuel was leaking. Soon there was an explosion, which destroyed the aircraft's rear section and caused a fire. The failure was caused by a broken turbine blade, which pierced the engine outer casing and fuel tank. The crew chief suffered burns. The aircraft was scrapped. On 26 October 1971, during an examination flight combined with ground target strafing at Jagodne gunnery, the engine of Lim-2 "1520" quit. The restart attempt failed and the pilot, Sgt Officer Cadet Jerzy Kislinger, ejected safely. The aircraft crashed 6 km away from Dęblin air base. Luckily, the mid-air collision of two Dęblin-based Lim-2s on 14 August 1972 claimed no casualties. Lim-2 "1604", flown Sgt Officer Cadet Jan Ptasiński, collided with "1516", flown by the instructor, 1st Lt Wacław Krukar. The flight controls of "1604" jammed, but the pilot ejected safely from his uncontrollable aircraft, which crashed near the village of Sarnów. 1st Lt Krukar managed to return to base in the damaged "1516" with the left fuel tank and nose crushed. In October 1972 the aircraft was transferred to No. 2 Military Aircraft Repair Works in Bydgoszcz. The undamaged rear section of "1516" was used for conversion of SBLim-1, (s/n 1A-07001), to an SBLim-2.

In the 61. LPSz-B the Lim-2s were used for training of officer cadets of the 3rd and 4th year until the 1980s. On 14 August 1962 a crash of Lim-2 "1111" took place. The engine failure caused a fire. The pilot, 1st Lt Lech Grajewski, jettisoned the canopy, but did not eject and died in the destroyed aircraft. Another Lim-2 crash took place on 5 September 1967. About one minute after the take-off from Nowe Miasto air base at night in good weather Lim-2 "1707" crashed and exploded about 4.5 km away from the airfield. The pilot, Sgt Officer Cadet Henryk Matyja, did not notice the descent and was killed. Five years later, on 29 September 1972, another Lim-2 crash took place. 1st Lt Walerian Józefacik was killed during his first solo night flight in bad weather with the use of the blind landing system after a years' recess. The pilot lost spatial orientation and Lim-2 "1512" crashed and exploded with the pilot in the cockpit 7 km away from Nowe Miasto air base. In the next crash on 6 March 1974 2nd Lt Andrzej Ślęzak was killed in Lim-2 "1823" during a training sortie above the overcast with the use of the blind landing system. The weather conditions were too bad for the pilot's skill level. The aircraft crashed 2.3 km away from the airfield. During one week in 1975 three crashes, claiming the lives of four pilots, took place in the 61. LPSz-B. On 27 June during a training sortie in good weather the CS-102 "634" with the crew 2nd Lt Kazimierz Łęgiecki and Sgt Officer Cadet Piotr Buczek collided in the air with Lim-2 "1930". Both the Lim-2 pilot, Sgt Officer Cadet Stanisław Wieczorek, and the CS-102 crew were killed. On 4 July Sgt Officer Cadet Bogdan Borkowski was killed in Lim-2 "1617" during his first solo medium flying training sortie. In late October 1977 the regiment was moved from Nowe Miasto to the expanded Biała Podlaska air base. In the autumn of 1977 in the regiment's inventory were about 80 Lim-2 and 25 SBLim-2 aircraft, although the regiment's lineup called for 48 aircraft. In the next year a large group of officer cadets arrived for Lim-2 conversion. The number of groundcrews was insufficient for servicing such a large

158

[158]: Lim-2 "1823" (s/n 1B-01823) in the 45. PLM OPL. Babimost air base, 1961. The soldier leaning against of the aircraft is Wacław Hołyś. This aircraft was lost in the 61. LPSzB in a crash on 6 March 1974.

[159]: Lim-2 "1912" (s/n 1B-01912) in the 62. PLM, based at Krzesiny.

159

1912

[160]: Lim-2 "1919" (s/n 1B-01919) in the 31. PLM based at Łask. On 7 November 1957 a pilot of this regiment, 1st Lt Bohdan Kożuchowski, hijacked it and made an emergency belly landing in the Halland region in Sweden.

number of aircraft. The groundcrews had to work in excess to keep the weary Lim-2s (and SBLim-2s too) flying. The crew chiefs were always able to prepare a sufficient number of aircraft for the training sorties. In the spring of 1980 conversion of another large group of cadets of the third year of Officer Flying Training School began. The last Lim-2 crash in Poland took place on 22 October 1980. During a sortie involving a practice gun camera attack on a manoeuvring aircraft Lim-2 "615", flown by Cpl Officer Cadet Bogusław Sidoruk, went into a spin and crashed between the villages of Wisznice and Rozwadówka-Folwark. The pilot ejected at low altitude and was killed. The aerobatic team "*Rombik*" (Diamond) on four Lim-2s represented the 61. LPSz-B for many years at various airshows nationwide.

During 1963–1980 ten Lim-2 aircraft ended service in the 61. LPSz-B due to failures or irreparable damage. "1828", "1904" and "811" crashed after the pilots had ejected. "1104", which hit the ground with the fuselage and caught fire in a botched landing, was scrapped. Lim-2R "924" (s/n 1B-00924), damaged after excessive g load in flight, was sent to No. 2 Military Aircraft Repair Works in Bydgoszcz. The aft fuselage section was used for conversion of CS-102 s/n 522514 to SBLim-2 "514". (The SBLim-2 "514" was destroyed in 1978 in a crash in Świdwin-based 40. PLM-Sz). The overhaul of obsolete "401" and "1517", damaged in a collision on the ground in 1974, was deemed uneconomical and they were written off. "313", "819", and "1426", heavily damaged in botched landings, were scrapped.

When Lim-2 production started in 1954, nineteen production batches were planned. The first four batches were to consist of 20 aircraft each and the subsequent batches were to be larger, with 30 aircraft in each. According to such a plan, 530 Lim-2 aircraft would have been built. About the fulfilment of this plan, various pieces of information can be found in publications from 1989, among others the one that 498 or 500 Lim-2 aircraft were built in 19 batches. Interventions and disinformation from censorship are possible. In 1989 information that Lim-2 production lasted until 23 November 1956 was published. It was stated that on that day the 500th Lim-2 aircraft (s/n 1B 01914), left the WSK Mielec factory and the assembly lines switched to Lim-5 production. However, Lim-2 production did not cease that day. Probably the 501st aircraft built at Mielec was "1915" (s/n 1B-01915). Along with "1915", aircraft from the 19th batch with subsequent numbers, "1917", "1920", "1921", "1922" and "1930", were assigned to the 39. PLM, based at Mierzęcice. It is also known that Lim-2 "1918" was in the inventory of the 11. PLM based at Debrzno. In early July 1957 further aircraft from the 19th batch with numbers above 1914 (1925–1931) were transferred from OSL-4 to Powidz-based 38. PLM. Probably "1931" (s/n 1B 01931) was built as the 517th Lim-2 aircraft. Specifying the actual number of the Lim-2 aircraft built is not possible due to the current state of the archive records and the fact of transferring documents to archives with various degrees of competence. Documents showing the entire Lim-2 production course are complete only until the end of 1953.

[161]: Lim-2 "1931" (s/n 1B-01931) of Powidz-based 38. PLM, built probably as the 517th example of this type. The photo was taken during formation assembly for an air parade. Modlin air base, September 1957.

[162]: Lim-2 "911" was often erroneously described as the Lim-2R fighter-reconnaissance variant. The expended cartridge case container was mistaken for a camera pod.

[163]: Lim-2 of Sochaczew-based 21. SPLR, seen in the background of the photo taken in May 1962. The aircraft wears a three-tone camouflage pattern on upper and side surfaces, consisting of yellow sand, green and gray sand. Lower surfaces were painted light blue up to half the fuselage's height. The tactical number "612" was red. The recognized pilots are 1st Lt E. Borowiak (second from left), and 1st Lt K. Zastawnik (with the arm band of the duty flight controller).

164 [164]: Lim-2 "112" (s/n 1B-01012) of the 10. PLM based at Łask. The aircraft is in natural metal (anodized duraluminium) finish, covered with transparent lacquer coating. The tank and tailfin tips are blue. The shape and size of the tactical number digits is atypical. The aircraft is fitted with PTB 300 underwing tanks and expended cartridge case container.

165 [165]: Lim-2 "112" (s/n 1B-01012) of the 10. PLM based at Łask. Note the large tactical number digits. The aircraft had blue tank and tailfin tips.

[166]: Lim-2 “410” (s/n 1B-00410) with PTB 400 underwing tanks. The aircraft is in natural metal (anodized duraluminium) finish, covered with transparent lacquer coating. The checkerboard on the starboard side of the fuselage has reversed colors.

[167+168]: Lim-2 “410” (s/n 1B-00410) with reversed colors of the checkerboard on the starboard side of the fuselage.

[169]: Lim-2 "806" (s/n 1B-00806) was operated during 1963–1968 in Sochaczew-based 21. PLRT. The red tactical number with shadow was applied before making an instructional movie about bailing out in the regiment. The aircraft remained in natural metal (anodized duraluminium) finish, covered with transparent lacquer coating.

[170+171]: Lim-2 "806" (s/n 1B-00806) with stylized tactical number, operated by Sochaczew-based 21. SPLR. During 28 December 1968 – 12 January 1971 this aircraft was assigned to 32. PLRTiA.

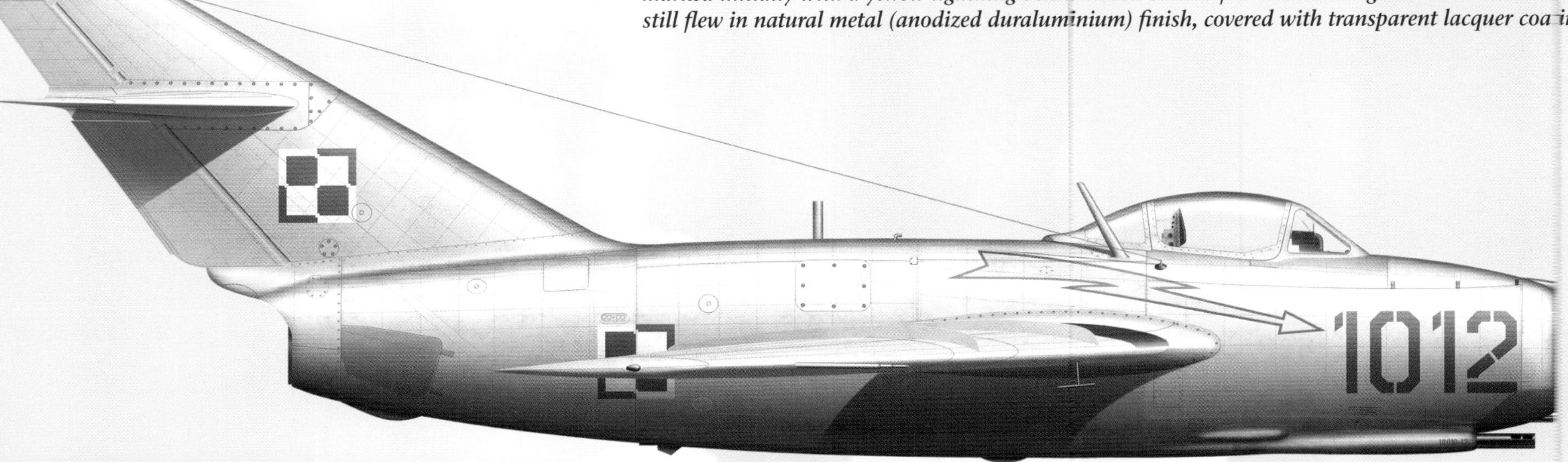

[172]: Lim-2 “1012” (s/n 1B010-12) of Capt. Ryszard Grundman from the 1. PLM “Warsaw”, in 1956 marked initially with a yellow lightning bolt with red outline for “outstanding aircrew”. The aircraft still flew in natural metal (anodized duraluminium) finish, covered with transparent lacquer coating.

[173]: Lim-2 “1012” (s/n 1B010-12) of Capt. Ryszard Grundman from the 1. PLM, in 1956, with an early marking of the “outstanding aircrew” in the form of a yellow lightning bolt with red outline.

[174]: Lim-2 “1306” (s/n 1B-01306) of the 31. PLM based at Łask, marked with a red lightning bolt of the “outstanding aircrew”. The aircraft is in natural metal (anodized duraluminium) finish, covered with transparent lacquer coating. Assembly before an air parade at Warsaw Bemowo/Babice airfield, 1959.

[176]: Lim-2 “1306” with altered shape of the tactical number digits.

[175]: Lim-2 “1306” (s/n 1B-01306) of the 31. PLM, marked with a red lightning bolt of the “outstanding aircrew” at the assembly of the 5. DLM OPL before the air parade on 22 July 1959.

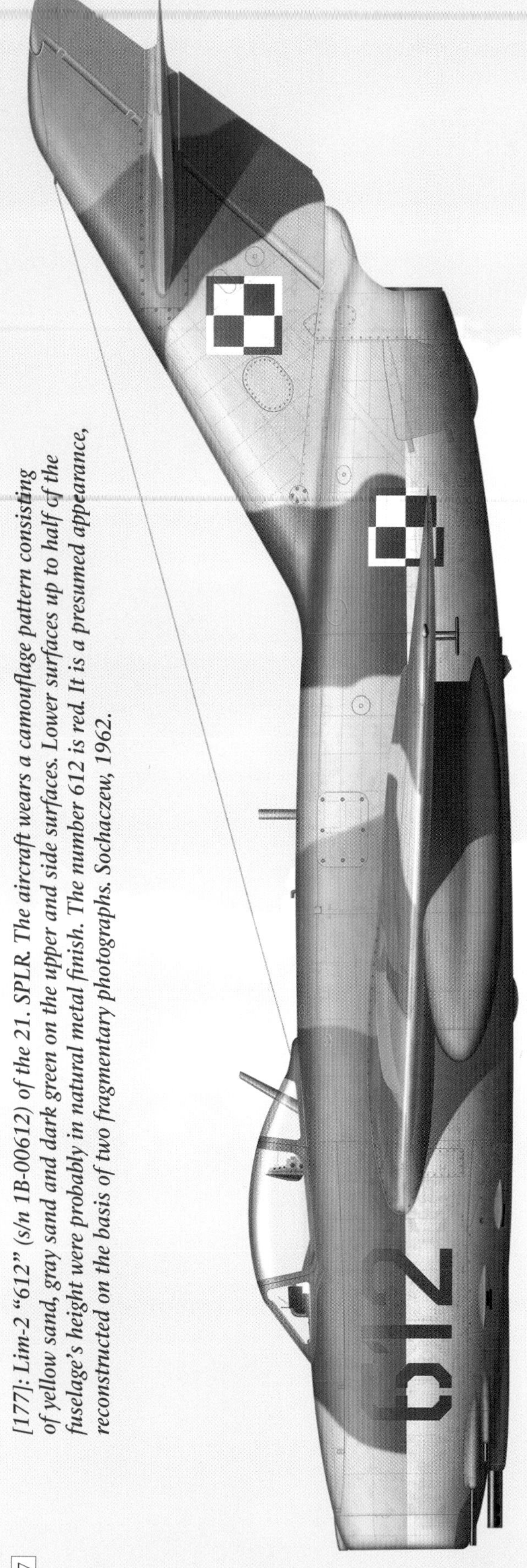

177

[177]: *Lim-2 "612" (s/n 1B-00612) of the 21. SPLR. The aircraft wears a camouflage pattern consisting of yellow sand, gray sand and dark green on the upper and side surfaces. Lower surfaces up to half of the fuselage's height were probably in natural metal finish. The number 612 is red. It is a presumed appearance, reconstructed on the basis of two fragmentary photographs. Sochaczew, 1962.*

178

[178]: *Lim-2 "612" (s/n 1B-00612) in the 21. SPLR is the second confirmed case of a similar camouflage pattern on a Lim-2. The tactical number visible is probably red.*

179 *[179]: Lim-2 "1214" (s/n 1B-01214) of the 45. PLM, based at Babimost. The aircraft is covered with silver/aluminium paint. For the duration of the exercise in 1961 a blue stripe was painted around the fuselage forward of the checkerboard.*

180 *[180]:Lim-2s "1214 and "1823" of Babimost-based 45. PLM. Blue stripes were painted around the fuselage for the duration of the exercise in 1961.*

Lim-2R (1B)

In the late 1950s and early 1960s in the air arm the demand for information about the disposition of mobile nuclear weapon delivery systems, introduced at the tactical/operational level, increased. Therefore efforts to increase the potential of the reconnaissance aviation were made. When more advanced MiG-17PF and licence-built Lim-5 and Lim-5P fighters entered service in the Polish air arm, it was decided to modify the Lim-2 fighters for the reconnaissance role by retrofitting them with a photo camera. The modified aircraft were designated Lim-2R. The armament was reduced to two NR-23 cannons. In No. 2 Military Aircraft Repair Works in Bydgoszcz the photo camera was installed in the gun tray. During take-off, cruise and landing the lens was covered with a sliding cover, which opened for the photo run. To make room for the camera, the 37 mm ammunition box was removed from the tray. To avoid shifting the centre of gravity aft, not all gun elements were removed from the tray. The 37 mm gun barrel remained in place on the right side of the lowering gun tray (which is visible in the photographs). The Lim-2R aircraft were retrofitted with AFA-BAF-21S photo camera, with 21 cm focal length. The camera could take up to 195 13x18 cm photographs from altitudes of 200–5000 m. It could take vertical single or series photos or oblique photos in a turn. In lieu of the camera a chaff dispenser could be installed. In Polish and English-language writing numerous authors had erroneously described photographs of Lim-2 aircraft with expended case containers as Lim-2Rs (e.g. "307", "911", "1004", "1123") or even the MiG-15bisF variant built in Poland… For several decades, when almost everything in the Polish military was secret, obtaining and publishing information about types, versions and equipment of the aircraft was impossible. Therefore speculations and false information about it were published.

The aircrew conversion to Lim-2 aircraft in the 21. PLR (*Pułk Lotnictwa Rozpoznawczego* – Reconnaissance Aviation Regiment) began in 1955. In November the regiment was renamed 21. SPLR. In 1956 the regiment consisted of four squadrons. The 3rd and 4th Long Range Reconnaissance Squadrons were equipped with the Il-28 (10 Il-28s and four Il-28Rs). The 1. and 2. EBR (1st and 2nd Short Range Reconnaissance Squadrons) had 20 Lim-2 and Lim-2R. On the occasion of the 550th anniversary of the victorious battle with the Teutonic Order the celebrations and air parade were held at Grunwald (Tannenberg) on 17 July 1960. Aircrews of the 21. SPLR took part in the parade. The lead aircraft of the parade, an Il-28, was assisted by four 2. EBR pilots on the Lim-2R: 2nd Jan Podkowiński, 2nd Lt Eugeniusz Borowiak, 2nd Lt Zbigniew Jędrzejewski and 2nd Lt Kazimierz Zastawnik. The leading Il-28 bomber was piloted by the commander of the 33. PLB (*Pułk Lotnictwa Bombowego* – Bomber Aviation Regiment), Maj. Jerzy Adamiec. During a night sortie of a Lim-2R from the 1. EBR on 5 July 1961, just after take-off 1st Lt Zbigniew Molak felt a vicious jerk of the aircraft and sudden turn to the left. The right underwing tank fell off. Smoke penetrated the cockpit, hampering reading the flight instruments. The pilot initially decided to climb and eject, but then, despite problems with flying the aircraft he chose not to bail out and decided to make an emergency landing. The landing was successful and the aircraft was not damaged. During a day four-ship formation flight in bad weather on 23 October 1963 a crash of the Lim-2R (s/n 1B-00709) took place. The task consisted of photographing objects in the town of Brześć Kujawski from below the overcast. 1st Lt Zygmunt Gruszczyk lost spatial orientation during climbing through the clouds. The Lim-2R "709" crashed in the village of Skrzynki near Gostynin. The pilot was killed. The short flight of the Lim-2R "1321" on 25 June 1964, which caught fire just after take-off from Sochaczew air base, had a happy end. When the aircraft was still visible from the airfield, flame behind it was observed. On the orders of the ground controller the pilot climbed, turned back and landed with the engine off. A piece of fuselage skin was burnt. The aircraft was repaired and returned

[181]: Lim-2Rs "114" and "508" during an aerial reconnaissance competition.

181

182

183

[182]: Lim-2R "502" photographed in 1958, when operated by the 34. PLM MW.

[183]: Lim-2 "606" (s/n 1B006-06) of the 21. PLRT based at Sochaczew before conversion to a Lim-2R.

184

[184]: Lim-2 "606" (s/n 1B006 06) of the 21. PLRT, after modification made in No. 2 Military Aircraft Repair Works in Bydgoszcz.

[185]: Lim-2R "706" of the 21. SPLR photographed in 1958.

[186]: Lim-2R "806", "709" and "804" and Lim-2 "612" on the flightline of the 21. SPLR at Sochaczew in 1956. The Lim-2R "709" was lost in a crash on 3 October 1963.

[187]: Lim-2R "804" (s/n 1B-00804) with different, larger digits of the tactical number, used in the later period of service in the Sochaczew-based regiment.

to service. According to the account of Lt Col. Tadeusz Chrobak, who joined the regiment in April 1963 as second lieutenant and soon began to fly the Lim-2 and Lim-2R aircraft, in the autumn of 1964 an unfortunate event took place in the unit. During a sortie a pair of Lim-2R aircraft descended below the ordered altitude without authorization. In the low-level flight the Lim-2R "1330" hit a high voltage line. The forward fuselage was cut apart to the 4th frame and several meters of wire stuck in the hole. Luckily, there was no crash and both aircraft returned safely to base. The two pilots wer e punished for "air hooliganism". The "1330" was repaired and returned to service. In 1969 the regiment was moved to Powidz. The "1330" was in trouble for the second and last time on 21 September 1970. On that day, during a sortie from Powidz air base, the Lim-2R "1330" flown by 2nd Lt Stefan Rogalski collided in the air with another Lim-2R, "120" (s/n 1B-00120), flown by Capt. Tadeusz Augustyn. After the collision both pilots ejected successfully and the aircraft collided again and crashed in the village of Helenów near Konin. On a single day two Lim-2Rs "120" and "1330" were lost.

The Lim-2 and Lim-2R aircraft were also in the inventory of the 32. PLRTiA (*Pułk Lotnictwa Rozpoznania Taktycznego i Artyleryjskiego* – Tactical Reconnaissance and Artillery Spotting Regiment), formed in 1963 at Sochaczew. In May that year three Lim-2 aircraft with tactical numbers "1120", "1305" and "1605", taken over from Bydgoszcz-based 48. PLM-Sz, were assigned to this unit. In May further Lim-2s, "708", "711", "715", "1501" and "607", were assigned to the unit. In 1968 both Sochaczew-based regiments were renamed 21. and 32. PLRTiA. During 1963–1968 thirteen Lim-2 and Lim-2R aircraft were taken over from the 21. PLRTiA.

In 1969 one squadron of the 21. PLRTiA, operating Lim-2R aircraft, was left in Sochaczew and attached to the 32. PLRTiA. Alomg with the new pilots 12 Lim-2 and Lim-2R aircraft were assigned to the regiment: "109", "111", "120", "801", "806", "1330", "1426", "1503", "1606", "1611", "1614" and "1729". On 26 August 1969, during a sortie for visual and photographic reconnaissance of simulated nuclear attack at Muszaki bombing range, Lim-2R "1611" (s/n 1B-01611) was lost. Upon accomplishment of the mission 1st Lt Jan Smutrykowski was directed to Modlin air base due to bad weather. At Modlin, in equally bad weather, in heavy rainfall and a low cloud base, attempts were made to guide the pilot to the runway. When only 100 liters of fuel was left, the pilot climbed to 2,000 m. Soon the fuel gauge showed zero and the pilot safely bailed out. He landed by parachute on a small island on the Vistula river. The aircraft went into spin and crashed 1 km away from the Modlin air-

188

[188]: Lim-2R "824" (s/n 1B-00824) during its service in the Sochaczew-based regiment. Before conversion it flew as Lim-2 "824" in the 4. PLM.

[189]: Lim-2R "924" of the 61. LPSz-B during an aerial reconnaissance exercise in 1971. After being damaged in 1972 it was sent to WZL-2 (No. 2 Military Aircraft Repair Works), when it was used for conversion to an SBLim-2.

189

[190]: Lim-2R "1126" during winter operations at Sochaczew air base.

[191]: Lim-2R "1416" (s/n 1B01416) z 21. PLRT. The lowering gun tray of distinctive shape, mounting the photo camera, is visible. After the service in the reconnaissance aviation regiment it was operated by the 53. PLM-Sz based at Mirosławiec.

[192]: Lim-2R "1503" (s/n 1B-01503) served as a fighter reconnaissance aircraft first in the 21. PLRTiA and during 28 December 1968 – 19 December 1969 in the 32. PLRTiA, also based at Sochaczew.

field. The training sorties on 10 July 1970 were interrupted by an a crash. On that day sorties for reconnaissance of the target, which was a four-gun battery, simulating an enemy artillery position located near the village of Gąbin near Konin, were undertaken. After the flypast over the spotted target 2nd Lt Adam Harabasz made a steep banking turn towards the target. The Lim-2R "415" (s/n 1B-00415) lost altitude, hit the ground and exploded. (The Lim-2 "415" (s/n 1B-00415) was converted during the medium overhaul in 1964 to the Lim-2R reconnaissance variant). During 1963–1972 a total of 28 Lim-2 and Lim-2R aircraft went through the inventory of the 32nd Regiment.

The Lim-2R aircraft converted from twenty-two Lim-2 fighters were as follows: "114", "120", "415", "502", "508", "606", "706", "709", "711", "804", "824", "924", "1126", "1321", "1330", "1416", "1503", "1527", "1606", "1611", "1614" and "1930".

During 1955–1980 a total of 79 Lim-2 and Lim-2R aircraft were lost in crashes. Failures, heavy damage and unprofitability of the overhaul caused the loss or scrapping of a 38 aircraft of this type...

193

194

[194]: Lim-2R "1611" (s/n 1B-01611) served in the 21. PLRTiA till 28 December 1968. Then it was transferred to the 32. PLRTiA, where it was lost on 26 August 1969 when flying in bad weather. The pilot bailed out.

[193]: Lim-2R "1614" (s/n 1B-01614) of the 21. PLRTiA in 1966.

Camouflage and Markings

Polish MiG-15, -15bis, Polish and Czechoslovak-built licence fighters left the factories in natural duraluminum finish except for the air brakes and steel gun blast shields. They were covered with transparent lacquer coating apart from the gun blast shields near the cannon muzzles. Individual batches of anodized duraluminium skin sheets differed significantly in gloss between each other. The aircraft received the homogenous silver paint scheme after the first overhaul, when an aluminium paint coating was applied. Walkways on the upper wing surfaces near the fuselage were painted dark grey. In some units the assignment of the aircraft was marked with a colourful vertical stabilizer tip. In the 1. PLM the stabilizer tip was red, in the 10. PLM blue and in the 13. PLM green. Sometimes the underwing tank tips were painted in the same colours. During exercises white or yellow stripes were often painted around the aft fuselage sections. The rules of marking the aircraft with tactical numbers were described in chapters covering individual versions. The variety of shapes of the tactical number digits, painted on the MiG-15s, MiG-15bis, S-102s, Lim-1s and Lim-2s, is shown in the photographs. In the 1950s Lim-2 aircrew who won the title "Outstanding aircrew" had the right to paint a red lightning bolt on both sides of the fuselage, below the cockpit. The Lim-2 "520" of the CO of the 61. LPSz-B, based at Nowe Miasto, had the nose section atypically painted red. In the early 1960s the Lim-2 "612" was painted in a multi-colour camouflage pattern, which is confirmed by the photo taken in the 21. SPLR based at Sochaczew. Another photo of a camouflaged Lim-2, visible in the background on the flightline, was taken in the Sochaczew-based regiment in 1962. This interesting photo does not allow us to ascertain whether it is the same "612" or another Lim-2 wearing a camouflage pattern.

195 [195]: Lim-2R "1614" (s/n 1B-01614) of the 21. PLRTiA in 1966.

[196]: Lim-2R “1606” (s/n 1B016 06) was also operated by two reconnaissance aviation regiments. First it was with the 21. PLRTiA and during 4 January 1968 – 7 March 1972 it was assigned to the 32. PLRTiA from which it was transferred to the 58. LPSz-B.

[197]: Lim-2R “1606” (s/n 1B016 06) of the 21. PLRT, Sochaczew 1966. (During the period of the regiment’s stationing in Sochaczew it was the fourth of five names of this unit). The aircraft was covered with silver/aluminium paint after conversion to the reconnaissance variant.